OFFICIAL MAINE STAYCATION MANUAL

official

maine

staycation

manual

by
DENA RIEGEL

illustrated by
Eric Hou

Down East

Text Copyright © 2011 by DenaRiegel
Illustration Copyright © 2011 by Eric Hou
All rights reserved.

ISBN: 978-0-89272-974

Library of Congress
Cataloging-in-Publication
Data available upon request.

Design by Jennifer Baum
Cover Design by Lynda Chilton

Cover Photography by: Ari Meil, Jason P. Smith, Amy Wilton

Printed in the United States of America

5   4   3   2   1

Down East
Books • Magazine • Online
www.downeast.com
Distributed to the trade
by National Book Network

contents

The Mission, Should You Choose to Accept it...

Lots of people want to be in Maine. You're probably here right now (or perhaps you wish you were). You'd think a person lucky enough to live here year-round would always appreciate access to 3,478 miles of coastline, award-winning restaurants, and postcard-perfect towns. Did you know we have 2,000 islands?

But sometimes we forget. No matter where we live – even in Vacationland – we sometimes stop seeing the swimming hole down the road, the downtown bakery, and the fairy houses in our own backyards. How did we let this happen? It's time to shed any indifference that may have accumulated for the beautiful place you live, and jog your enthusiasm for things you love to do. This advice will work no matter where you live. A great staycation is achievable in any city and any town, but, as any self-respecting Maine resident will tell you, a staycation is best in Maine!

Visitors come to Maine and see things we don't. I walked the streets of Portland – my day-to-day town – with a friend "from away" and stopped in surprise when he said, "Wow. You guys like to eat and do yoga, huh?" I suddenly had the eyes of a tourist with the soul of a denizen. Wonder for my city was renewed. I thought, "Oh, my gosh. These sidewalks are all brick! How beautiful! Would you look up at that late-Victorian architecture?" Love for my particular city, full of fishermen, restaurant workers, lawyers, artists, teachers, and, yes, yoga instructors, came rushing in. I thought about how some of us frequent farmers' markets. Many like early morning greasy-spoon rituals of coffee and shooting the breeze. A lot of us drink microbrews or go to see all kinds of live shows, from blues to burlesque, from Irish to rock, modern plays to symphonies. I realized that I have the "inside information" every tourist pursues. So does everyone in their respective towns with their own local wonders - but I'm partial to Maine. It's full of tourist-worthy, as well as the subtle and the undersung, wonders—and we don't have to book a flight to get to them. A cappuccino in Portland is on par with one in Paris. A walk to a park with your dog, throwing a tennis ball into the waves, is an afternoon well-spent. Eating a fresh bagel with melting butter from a cozy closet of a bakery makes your Thursday.

Even if you're vacationing locally out of financial necessity, concentrating on your community can help you discover that pleasure in life has less to do with money and more with putting yourself in the right situations. It's in finding pockets of fun and flavor that you would pass by if you were in a faster lane. Thinking we always need "something else" isn't a healthy way for anyone to try and relax! Less can often mean less bother. There is an abundance right here, local, and waiting for you.

This book is a fun-instigator, like your favorite aunt or friend to turn to when you're bored, uninspired, or just not doing any of those interesting things you dream about. Some suggestions get specific, like recipes and real geographical nooks and crannies in Maine for you to explore. Other ideas are quieter little moments that will have you wondering, "Why don't I do this more often?" Feel free to open to any random page when you get stuck in an Internet whirlpool and need real-world escape—and scribble in the margins to add to the creative broth. Think of it as a kind of Yellow Pages—listings to keep you from listlessness.

The mission of this book is to help us to love the lives that we're living right now. Not appreciating our beautiful state doesn't mean Maine's not giving us what we need; it means we've forgotten to open our closed shutters, to run around in its green forests, to pick a crisp flannel shirt off the line, to make a sandwich for an adventure on the water. It's time to remember.

Welcome to Staycationland.

Left Instead of Right:

Turning an Explorative Way Instead of the Most Direct and Familiar Way

This idea was made most famous by Robert Frost, and I encourage you to take it quite literally in your awaiting endeavors. As a kid, my mischievous mother would ask me and my sisters on the way home from the grocery store, "Okay: left or right?" and we'd have a "choose-your-own-adventure" ride home. Whereas this freaked my little sister out and she acquired a perfect internal compass as she grew up from the fear of getting lost, I loved it, and the concept has stuck with me. These are little bites throughout the book that you can grab and go when you need a quick idea and want to go down an unplanned path.

"Two roads diverged in a wood, and I—
I took the one less traveled by,
And that has made all the difference."
                                        -*Robert Frost*

CHAPTER 1

What's a Staycation?

stay-ca-tion – noun:
a vacation spent at home or nearby
origin:
blend of stay and vacation
First known use:
2005

Staycations got their big break from humble means. Increased interest in exploring and supporting the local economy, an ailing national economy (the decline of which historically lines up with the concept's invention), and hiked-up gas prices are more than enough reasons for Mainers to kick back and relax where they are. The staycation trend may have been sparked by economic necessity, but it's gone forth and prospered because it's blood-pressure-lowering and fun.

Honestly, it can be more fun than a traditional vacation. Sleep-deprivation seating on your flight, long lines, stopovers, and bad airport food costs the same as a four-star meal for two and a night on the town. On a staycation, you funnel money, usually spent on cramped, uncomfortable travel, towards luxuries you couldn't otherwise afford. You don't have to worry about recycled flu-ridden air in a plane, nor the adjustments and settling of hotel rooms, travel hangups, the kind-but-clueless concierge telling you that they have "no reservation on record" and you have effectively traveled 800 miles to sleep in a bed-bug motel down the road. Perhaps I exaggerate. But what isn't an exaggeration is how potentially stressful travel is. Also, consider the travel time, as well as the recovery time upon arrival, as time you can use instantly in your staycation.

A staycation highlights the wonder in the familiar because it's the best of the basics. It's blueberry jam on a Maine-made popover or an ice cold beer on a seaside porch restaurant. It's why we love things like line-fragrant cotton sheets, growing our own indecently plump vine tomatoes, and french-press breakfasts in bed. The domestic life is the good life.

Think of it this way: what's the last, best day you had? I doubt it involved collating an enormous office mail-out or updating your professional contact list. Was it sharing gossip and a bottle of frosty white wine with a friend from out of town? When your neighbors dropped by in their pajamas on a Sunday afternoon with muffins, and all your kids made blanket forts in the living room with Puff the Magic Dragon as a babysitter, and you all ended up dancing in the kitchen? Was it sitting by the lake or beach with your sweetie, mint iced-tea and a bodice-ripper novel your only other company?

We all have our different definitions of paradise.

What makes these moments special is what makes the advice of this little manual pertinent. The common thread in those different staycations is that the have-to's (or "havetas," as my mom says) are blissfully absent. When on vacation, you should focus on "wannas," not "havetas."

So then, how do you get the luster of a vacation while being around "mundane" surroundings? And, in a place where there are presumably multiple "havetas" staring you down? Therein lies the problem: our surroundings are mundane because we don't prioritize fun, spontaneity, and relaxation within them. We live in "Vacationland"; don't you think we should know how to vacation? As a goal, we should exhale "This is the Life!" more frequently than not. We should also give a thought to what we mean by that.

The Life: it's referenced enough to be a common idiom at this point. What is it? When do we recognize it and feel most alive? Perhaps it's an offhand comment of general happiness, but there is a profound depth of presence in the sentiment. We love those moments because our minds are engaged and blissfully drinking in new tastes, paths, people—or maybe we're just soaking up some needed sun, for goodness sakes. When we're amidst our obligations, pleasures seem hard to accomplish—or unlikely. We squander the precious hours we have with necessity instead of pleasure because we have trained ourselves to live by all or nothing: we're either in our "normal life" or "on vacation." What about "the Life"— the only one you have—and what you wish to fill it up with? A staycationing mindset puts the fun back in your function, and allows some room to scatter pleasures throughout your day.

Prioritizing good times (idle entertainment like internet and TV are not included here) takes some thought. When managed right, handling the necessities of life can create a harmony and natural rhythm to our days that lets us relax in those moments we allow ourselves, knowing that our obligations have been handled. As short as a day is, there are a lot of minutes in it. This book is for those moments in between as well as the staycation you want to plan. Adventure is completely attainable. Your town and your state can feel like a real vacation whenever you need one.

Why Staycation?

Avoid Baked-on Travel Feeling
Your vacation doesn't need to include recycled air or over-priced airport food when you're close to home. You'll feel (and smell) fresh upon arrival at your staycation destination.

Be Cheap, Cheap, Cheap
The money you save on gas now goes toward herb-crusted salmon at a restaurant you've been dying to try. The money you save on plane tickets can now go towards ferry tickets (to a Maine island!), and dinner and bike rentals and... There are many ways not to spend money on a vacation. It sometimes takes more planning than you would prefer, but you also won't get a credit card statement at the end of your sojourn that puts you into a cold sweat. (More on this later.)

Rewrite Your Perception
When hiccups in plans inevitably occur while on a vacation, you're more inclined to think "It's all part of the experience" rather than a frustrating disruption of your good time. Anyone who has waited two hours for a Costa Rican bus, but polished up their Spanish with a local because of it, has this kind of a relationship with inconvenience. Staycationing gives you permission to take on a laissez-faire attitude in surroundings you might usually try to control.

Renew Your Sense of Wonder
Uprooting ourselves brings out our best qualities. We don't explore when we think we already know everything about the world we're living in. Exploring makes us present and creates that relaxing feeling of wonder we so desperately seek out when on a vacation. It's what makes us wander down that brick alley that isn't on the way to anything, or follow the old salty shopkeeper's advice for seeking out the freshest hake in the Gulf of Maine. There is the aspect of other people, the world, which we are "safe from" when we choose not to interact. But a stranger's new puppy can make us smile. Four snowflakes on our sleeve can create an entire world of images and inspiration—visions of cocoa, borrowed fireplaces, that ski trip we want to schedule. Challenge yourself to do something you don't quite feel like doing—just be sure it's fun!

Rediscover the Romance of Your Hometown

The same activity, when done in a different environment, takes on an attitude. Writing in a journal amid our screaming children is switched to writing in a journal and people-watching in that coffee shop with all the hip-looking urbanites in it. Eating a sandwich on the graffitied picnic table outside your office building parking lot is flipped when you are instead eating a foot-long Italian sub with salt, pepper, and oil by the fountain in the park five minutes away. They make your life more romantic in subtle, but tangible, ways. I'm not sure if you need a cinema reference here – try *Groundhog Day*, *The Majestic*, or *It's a Wonderful Life*—but the concept of rekindled small-town romance has a substantial cinematic budget to back it up.

Rekindle Your Passion – for Your hobby, Your family, Your life

Campfire songs on your guitar, planting irises along your entrance path, finally cooking that macaroni and cheese that has two pounds of cheddar (you've put it off long enough). Your relationships—to the things that make you tick and the people that make you smile—are about to come out of storage.

Get Slower, Faster

Once you cut out the travel days, you can take a full-fledged vacation without taking much time off work. A staycation allows you to have more fun in less time so you can hit the ground running—or maybe skipping.

Why Do You Need a Staycation?

What are your top three reasons for taking a staycation? Three is a nice, neat number to help keep your eyes on the prize, so to speak. A lot of folks are inclined to take a wanderlust approach when dreaming up a vacation. They've been to Peru, Spain, and New Zealand in their minds, but what they actually need is some R&R: something they wouldn't have much time for while trekking around the globe! It's good to rein it in with a solid Top 3 before expanding out. Financial reasons is usually a big one, and that is completely okay. You're among friends. Admitting that will help you to stay realistic about what's in store. (I'll talk more about financial plans later.)

What else is on your list? Do you miss gardening? Do you have a long list of restaurants you've been wanting to try? Do you love poker night because you can be yourself and have a beer? What do you love about your life and living in Maine? Maybe you love it when your kids go on sleepovers because you get to take a bath and read trashy gossip magazines. Set some priorities, and maybe some needed limits, and make sure what you really want is represented.

What Have You Been Missing?
A Few Possible Lists:
Sleep
Romantic time
Cooking for fun instead of necessity

Films & live theater
Live sports
Running around outside

Restaurant tour
Time with family
Visiting weird roadside attractions on Route 1

Lasting Reasons to Staycation

These tweaks to your "normal" behavior seem easy, but they do take that extra leap and bit of commitment to carry out. Be ready to dare yourself. The fun thing in a staycation is the unexpected—not knowing what you'll learn, who you'll see, and the thrill of the different. You won't get it at home with your cat.

Best of all, the time you spend vacationing here is also time spent building profound and lasting relationships with the landscapes, holes-in-the-walls, and your own favorite stretches of twisty-turny backroads. There was a time, in recent history, when most Maine honeymooners went camping. I'm sure this is part of the reason so many of us have wonderful family-owned camps now; these couples could reminisce and romance in a honeymoon spot year after year. It became a part of their identity, their relaxing oasis a bit off the map. These couples probably stayed close to home out of financial necessity, too. A lot of us have that in common. Somewhere along the line, our definition of vacation came to mean "far away." But the encouraging evidence remains that we didn't used to have to go far away to "get away." Everything we need has always been right here.

CHAPTER 2

Get Ready, Get Set, Go!

How You Relax:
The Truth Will Set You Free

Some people feel their most relaxed hosting a brunch on a summer Sunday. They zen out as they pour their friends iced coffee, chat about politics, children's dance recitals, upcoming parental visits, and chop onions to add to sizzling butter waiting in a hot skillet.

For other people, this exact scenario above gets the heart racing and an innocent guest's inquiry of "Where's the half and half?" elicits a snappy, unnecessarily curt response from the gracious host.

When it comes to planning brunch, please be honest with yourself. That means accepting that if watching your friends eating off your china freaks you out, maybe going out is a better idea. When it comes to planning your staycation, it means making sure you focus on *what you want* and *haven't been getting*.

If you are a chronic over-scheduler, give yourself down-time with limited exertion. Space that out amid much-needed calm, of one kind or another (book reading and slow walks). If you feel bored with your day-to-day, have suddenly seen yourself thirty pounds heavier in a bathing suit, and really need a playful kick in the pants, go do something that feels a little scary, active, and maybe younger than you feel. Dancing, an art class, or belting out karaoke could be what you need.

When you are in the midst of staycation prep-work and taking an honest look at what you need, keep in mind that both vacations and staycations are done with the intention to escape "normal," boring ruts of behavior—to put on your Hawaiian shirt, metaphorically speaking. Letting your freak-flag wave allows you to experience life like a bug-chasing kid again. Your point in staycationing isn't to up and abandon your dull khaki-and-tan life for one of Caribbean blue: it is to make your *life* Caribbean blue. You're going to have to be a little brave here.

Small, Brave Moves

What makes you uncomfortable, but has always fascinated you anyway? The concept of comfort can mean a lot of different things, depending on who you are. Being brave looks bigger or smaller, depending on your personal limits. Some people were just born more adaptable than others: they speak fluent French after their second café au lait in Montreal, and they know how to get caustic in-laws purring. For creatures of habit, "wingin' it" may be adding garlic salt to their daily egg-salad sandwich. That's okay, too, for you wild egg-salad eaters out there.

If you're a young, hip urbanite, go somewhere that has bean suppahs and wooly sweaters in a western-Maine Elk's lodge. If you feel like you're too old for a scene, put on a dark shirt and go anyway as an art critic or a designer. Artists, as a rule, can be older, on the scene, and totally accepted. Hey, I say fake it till you make it if it brings you another perspective. Be brave.

> *What you're trying to do is to transform locations of stress-minefields into peaceful sanctuaries. Does the laundry room make you feel exhausted? What if you bring NPR and a glass of white wine down there with you? Inhale the Downy and take a moment for yourself.*

Staycation Home/ Home Staycation

There are two ways to approach planning your staycation. One is to figure out what you love about home and do it, staycation-style. The other is to figure out what you love about vacation and do it, homestyle.

Home, Staycation-style: *Act Like an Out-of-Towner*
Getting out of your rut sounds easy until you need to think of something different to do with your time. We all have our favorite spots, our safe havens and funtime sanctuaries. I'll be honest; it's wonderful to be a regular somewhere. But what if you were visiting yourself from out of town and wanted to impress...yourself? You

can really simplify this by thinking about where you take your friends when they come from out of town. When we're entertaining other people, we want them to see the best of the area, the greatest things our little corner of the world has to offer.

In Maine, we're often the elected good-natured sports that bring our friends out for a "real Maine" seafood dinner, bean suppah, or clambake on an inside-scoop "fire-friendly" beach. The reason we save our fun things for people we entertain is befuddling. Shouldn't we sometimes enjoy some of the good stuff ourselves?

My friend came to visit me over Christmas, and I showed her some fun! I was suddenly awash with activities and thoughts about what might keep her entertained and enjoying herself while we were in each other's treasured and rare presence. I brought her to Robinson's Woods in Cape Elizabeth, where we passed many Cape Elizabeth women wearing Patagonia jackets and enjoying this beautiful big back yard with their children. It had seemed just far enough away – *alllll* the way over the Casco Bay Bridge (a ten minute drive)—to keep me from discovery. Because my friend was with me, I treated us both to some local flavor at a local bakery and a snowy walk in the woods. I'm not sure I would have prioritized for myself in the same way I did for my friend. And why not?

That is the answer, in fact: Why not! This sort of planning needs to be necessary for you in your staycation. Where would you want your friend to take you on a visit? Take yourself there! Get the imported prosciutto for yourself. Get yourself a pedicure at that fancy place you last went to when your niece had her *bat mitzvah*.

Think Like You're Entertaining a Visiting Friend and List Your Favorites:
5 restaurants
5 parks/outdoor spaces you go for walks/views/sightseeing
5 events (movies, improv, theatre, outdoor concerts, etc.)
5 playing around (beaches, bowling, golf)
5 festivals, fairs, quirky local flair (yard sales, blueberry festivals, bean suppers, etc.)

Vacation, Homestyle

What gives that instant blood-pressure-lowering feel of a good vacation? Why do we thrive once we're "at ease" on a vacation? Maybe you allow other people to cook for you on a vacation. Maybe your rules fall away a bit; you're more likely to grab that eclair after wandering into the heavenly smells of a bakery from a leisurely walk, the buttery clouds filling your senses. Whim has taken you by the hand.

Think about your favorite vacation moments, especially those guided by friends. Everyone can use a suggestion: whether you know exactly what you want on your itemized clip-board of fun; you don't like to plan and would prefer to be lead; or you have a few pretty good ideas and are in need of some flourishes to pepper throughout your time. Copying someone else's great idea is a perfect place to start your staycation.

List your favorite vacation moments, what you loved about them, and how you could replicate them on a staycation. Examples: that morning you read the whole *New York Times* in your fluffy hotel bathrobe, drinking room service coffee – easy to replicate at home.

Get Ready

Avoiding Fun-suckers Like Chores and Menial Tasks

Our parents once created rules for us. They were meant to keep us safe from hot surfaces and the rest of the threatening world, to keep us reasonably hygienic, and to make sure we could function at an organized and creative level with our surroundings. "Turn off the TV" was a religious chant in my home, followed closely by the descant "Go outside!" So I turned away from the TV toward two childhood wonders: the big woods of my backyard and Barbies. Society may deem these two choices unlikely compliments, but to me, there was nothing like Barbies in the forest. Some rules are made to be broken. And others, like "Go outside," are just smart.

Now that you're all grown up and maybe have yowlins of your own, you make rules for your kids. But what kinds of rules do you hold for yourself? Maybe I'm preaching to the choir right now; maybe your iPhone is attached to your Kindle is attached to your laptop, and you know what you're doing every minute of the day. You don't need to know how to get things done (although, you may need to know how to unwind) and maybe you don't need this kind of advice from a fantasy-driven realist like myself. But for others, like me, who regretfully forgo the spinning class, egg-white omelette, work, Oprah's bookclub recommendation, and in bed by ten kind of lifestyle, a few rules must be laid out. These rules stabilize your loose schedule and give it a bit of structure to make sure you're not forgetting something. If you are among the weaker-willed—the easily seduced by a cuppa and reruns on Hulu ("fun-suckers" as I call them) or things that snap you out of your staycation time—and find you don't get quite enough done in a day, consider the following:

You're Not Available

A vacation lets us turn off our cell phones and tune out everything that isn't in the present moment. Most of us wouldn't dream of interrupting it with an email or office phone call. Why then do we prioritize interruptions into our daily lives so much? Being available to the world is great: we can get our best-friends' opinions by sending them a picture via iPhone of the ruffled blouse they saved us from purchasing. But unavailability these days is a political statement. I know people—you know who you are—who believe the construction of a peanut butter sandwich is newsworthy Facebook info. I was on a friend date recently, ready to enjoy the quality time we'd set aside, only to have it interrupted by the constant text messages my friend received during our beers, chats, and dinner. My quality time with her was being stolen via her over-availability! The time wasn't focused, and the "quality" of our time was certainly compromised when I had to share it with her Blackberry. What if she didn't answer her phone while we were out?

Why not choose to go through life more as a vacation than as an obligation to the ether of technology? When we are constantly "at the ready," it always feels like something is left undone. It's a constant flight or fight stance. Obligations bring tension to our chests—they make crowsfeet appear. They interrupt otherwise relaxed conversations with friends, neighbors, our children. They take us away from the bird song in the tree, the salty sea air in our lungs, the appreciation and feel of a hand-thrown piece of pottery in a cute local shop.

Organizing Your Time

When planning your staycation, write it all down. Make the lists mentioned in the book, and do it now, while you're thinking about it. You'll be more likely to do the things you say you love when they're in writing because writing makes them official, and keeps you from being distracted instead of intentional. Make a list with crayons or colors that make you smile a bit, or dictate to a child who's proud of writing. Cross things off as they're done. I swear to you, getting organized can be fun.

Doing Away with the "Dread"

If you're not convinced that it's important to get organized, stop to consider this necessary question: What do you want to return to? I'm willing to bet that you're not going to want to handle a dirty, cluttered home upon your return. Whether this return is from away or a return to reality within your abode, a neat space helps ease the pain of that "R" word we avoid at all costs when on vacation.

So: Clean. Your. House. Maybe you won't care while you're staycationing, but returning to kitty litter caked-on the bathroom tiles, unswept sidewalk salt on your living room's pine floors, and gross things now residing in your fridge won't make you think a staycation is ever worth it again. We escape these realities to relax and find freedom in our actions again: actions not weighed down by "should I," or "shouldn't I," but "because I wanna!" You won't be helping yourself if you leave your house in college-dorm hovel condition. Your "real life" will just seem all the more lackluster upon your return. This isn't the point. The *point* is to return the thrill of living into its rightful place: Every Single Day.

This part of preparation can be fun. Put on some great music everyone knows the lyrics to (Crosby, Stills, Nash, and Young's *So Far* does the trick for me). Give your kids, partner, or friends rags to put on their feet and have them mop the floor Pippi Longstocking-style. They'll never forget it. I know I haven't (thanks, Mom!). Use your kitchen timer as a wonderful count-down solution to make cleaning feel like a game. You'll be amazed at how much your five year old can get done in five minutes, or how many dishes you can do in seven. As for the laundry, pile everything together, and fold it up to more music or a so-bad-it's-good movie.

And if all else fails, there's always bribery. Offering your kids allowance for completed chores is an awesome way to contribute to your home's welfare and fresh scent, while giving today's lazy children (what's *with* kids today, huh?) some incentive to work their butts off for you. As a kid, I used to happily scrub the porcelain throne, knowing I would be richer for it. Remember to use nice-for-the-environment cleaning supplies; your toilet will be just as clean using vinegar as it would be from some fumey fluorescent blue gel that might give your grandchildren gills.

Or, if you have a little extra saved up, take your family out to a nice long brunch and arrange for elves to clean while you're away. A lot of cleaners can do a great job for eighty dollars, depending on the size of your house, and coming home to a sparkling house is a great way to kick off your staycation. Just be sure to check in with the cleaning service ahead of time about how much time they'll need!

Taking Care of Business

Have you paid your bills? Not something you want to think about while you're trying to relax. If you haven't already become friends with online banking; you're about to embark on a beautiful relationship. You can schedule automatic payments and ensure you don't have a forehead-smacking "NO!" moment when you're trying to unwind. Be sure all your stuff is taken care of before you go - make those lists again, if you need to! Just be sure that you send in the tax forms, give the field-trip permission slip, confirm the dentist appointment *before* you go (mentally or physically) away for a few days. No, it won't be the end of the world if you have to forward your new mailing address to your Michigan cousins for their upcoming/impending wedding while you're trying to be "away," but it might, for a minute, take away from your experience and, even more dangerously, lure you into a terrible, must-be-avoided-at-all-costs downward spiral of "to dos!" that could really make your staycation stink. I certainly won't make any kind of believer out of you if you are filling out auto insurance while you're trying to staycate. Please don't do it. Just don't. Save it for before or, if you must, after your staycation.

Calling All Workaholics

It's harder for you to sit still, your mind works a mile a minute, and you just want to "do something" most of the time. My insight into workaholics on vacation comes from places where urbanites go to unwind the most: the Hamptons, Martha's Vineyard, and posh Maine islands. I've overheard well-kempt couples discussing how the fast rules of the city don't apply in the Hamptons. I've watched a flock of silver-haired cyclists, just starting to warm up their cubicle pallors with sunburns, swerve around Vineyard Haven like ten year olds, whooping and ringing their bells. I've listened to summer people explain that they wear eccentric vacation hats to signify that they aren't in the city anymore and can finally relax. The rules change when you leave your datebook at the door. But what about leaving your datebook at the door when you don't actually *leave*?

We easily evade fun-suckers when we're somewhere else on a vacation. We can even sometimes do it around the holidays: Christmas and Hanukkah are sacred spaces for ourselves, family, and friends, and we sometimes just let the phone ring, let the chores wait for another day. That's what made the old term "holiday" such a great way to announce: "It's official, world: I'm going on a holiday."

Spreading the Word

Let friends, family, and coworkers know that you are on vacation! Set an "out of office" reply on your email, update your Facebook status to "away from the computer," and change your outgoing voicemail message so people know you'll only be responding to the most urgent matters. Tell coworkers and friends that you're away and can't be reached. Make that automatic message on your email say "Gone on Holiday! See you in a week!" They don't need to know you're on a ferry to Chebeague.

Stopping the Press (or not)

Consider stopping your mail and newspaper during your staycation. Try to make yourself as untouchable as you can. Current events are often troubling, and now is not the time for trouble. You can deal with rational thought and informed ideas when you get back. Now is time to put in front of you what you "wanna" know and "wanna" do, not necessarily what you think you should know and do. You're not an inconsiderate person; you're just going on vacation.

For those of you who long for lazy mornings with the *New York Times*, go for it! Just give some thought to what stresses you out and what allows you to relax.

All Together Now...

Nothing makes the heart sink faster (sometimes even before we *leave* for vacation!) than the idea of returning to "The Real World." The built-in risk of the staycation, and why people don't think to do it more, is that real-worldness easily creeps into the cracks of a vacation had in your every-day universe. You've got to mark your territory.

How do you keep from matching those pairs of socks you've been meaning to get to or taking that phone call? Or, God help you, working? The compulsory "havetas" sneak in whether or not you extend them an invitation. They must be kicked out of your party at all costs. That's why cleaning and doing all this prep work (that usually brings out the lazy teenager in all of us) is actually a great idea. When you return to your world, more relaxed than before, your transition will be peaceful and your resting will seem worth it.

You've definitely got to rein in your usual tendencies: turning on the TV or YouTube videos, calling people you've been meaning to call – unless they're ready to party on with Yahtzee and beer. You could make an exception, if it's something that makes you happy. Remember: prioritize what you haven't been getting in your life.

Get Set

The "B" word: Budget!

If you have lots and lots of money stuffed under your "rainy day" mattress, you are one smart and lucky hoarder. Now you just need to decide what to do with it! Many of us, however, need to think about how to spread the butter out on our slab of vacation toast. I mean, who isn't looking for a bigger bang per buck? Saving money for these kinds of things is a nice place to start—we're all trying to reach that goal of money-stuffed mattress staycation planning, aren't we?

A financial planner at Schwab once told me that he and his kids were saving up for a flatscreen by using a giant glass jar of pocket change. Yes, pocket change. He said, "If you save slowly to buy an object, you'll know it's a good decision if you still want it after all the wait." He elaborated about how much more satisfying purchases can be when there is anticipation, saving, and thought behind them. Figure out how much money you'll need for meals, outings, matching family argyle socks. Think about going "cash only," and setting aside stacks of bills in fun accordian-style folders to use for different stuff, like nights out, day trips, gas, and other categories you foresee as useful. One of the most well-traveled people I know uses this 1930s-esque style of money organization. Having your credit card bill undo all of the relaxing you've done is no way to wrap up a staycation.

Get Your Stock Ready!

Stock up on groceries and get your family favorites and special treats. Think about taking a poll for fanfare meals, and have family members pick their favorite dinners and make them together. (Remember, this is supposed to be fun. If your kid's favorite meal is Thanksgiving dinner and you hate to cook, ask a different leading question!)

Stock up on supplies, like games, sporting equipment, and charcoal. Make sure you have enough glue, watercolor paper, paint, scrapbook materials, and dress-up clothes. Replenish your stash of flippers, sand pails, and sparklers. Cram the pantry with plenty of cupcake papers, sugar, flour, and chocolate chips. This stuff won't go bad, and anything you can do to avoid a trip to the market or a big box store is worthwhile.

Want a different setting for your Staycation? Move the Furniture!

Nothing says "New Chapter!" quite like a different feng shui flow in your home or apartment. I hated my bedroom bad before we relocated our neatly folded clothing onto a lovely shelf system and moved our bed right next to the window. I love it now. Move your computer so you can see the birds. Move your pans to where you can reach them, and move your hankies to a lower shelf so you stop using the paper ones that are rough on your schnoz. Put the cupcake tins within reach so you make those chocolate cupcakes with the lemon icing more often. Move your couch to face the southern sun in winter and into a cool corner in the summer. Why is furniture stagnant in our minds? Let me tell you, you will be a changed person if you staycate in a rearranged home.

Now, go make some pumpkin pancakes with those easy-to-reach pans.

Those Little Touches

What are your favorite places to visit? A certain hotel? A lakeside B&B? Your uncle's house in Ogunquit? Think about the little luxuries that make you smile when you go to those special places and give them a try. Arrange fresh flowers in every room, perhaps. Stockpile mints to put on everyone's pillows every night. Get little sample sizes of toiletries. Replenish your stash of take-out menus. Trade your old towels for snow-white hotel-types that bring a little lasting luxury into your life.

Go!

So, you're finally ready for a little R&R. Any relaxation worth doing is worth doing well. Remember when we were kids, and grownups did things for us to help our little lives along? Teachers organized oceanic field trips, parents planned southwestern vacations, and Big Bird birthday parties were thrown in our honor. Being big has its perks, sure—we can go to bed whenever we want and can eat candy at our desks. But without the guidelines of childhood, how do we know when and how to have fun in our daily settings? It's not necessarily penciled into our day. Recess doesn't come after lunch. Music class doesn't show up to inspire us to clap our hands. We don't obediently board buses to go to the museum of science. "What we should do?" comes up all the time in friendly conversation, and it's ongoing. We've set the stage and made our homes beautiful: all we need now are suggestions.

Straightforward childhood rules like "go play outside!" as I mentioned earlier, and "recess is after lunch!" are excellent places to start. Keeping your schedule within "must play" guidelines is good for you. As for filling your playtime, begin an ongoing "fun list" for yourself as you overhear things in stranger's conversations at the café, or read about in magazine and newspapers. Cross things off as you go. You can look at all of those satisfying slash marks of your sharpie and know you've been somewhere and done something with your life. That said, I think it's wonderfully healthy and good for you to schedule in "Do Nothing" if that's what you've been missing! Include a plan for every day, even if it's a "just in case" list of fun stuff, and even if that plan is a whole lot of nothing... and margaritas.

Decorate an Idea Well
Turn a coffee can, fish bowl, vase, lunchbox, or some other equally distinguished vessel into an idea well! Have everyone write down a few ideas on scraps of paper and toss them in, then pull them out and DO THEM as the staycation unfolds. Need some idea-inspiraton?
- *Spend the afternoon at your favorite coffee shop – or a brand new one*
- *Hit Happy Hour at some friendly pubs*
- *Check the local rag for entertainment happenings*
- *Browse a general store*
- *Visit some artists' studios*
- *Read local bulletin boards for wild ideas!*

CHAPTER 3

Outdoor Activities

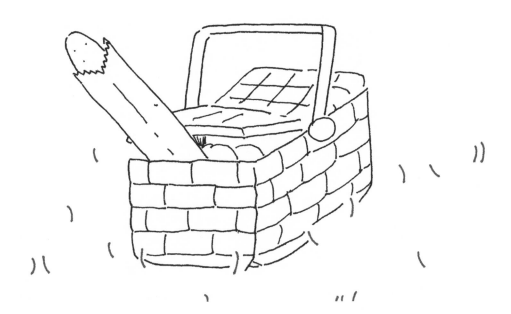

Take a Field Trip

Second only to the rush of the Halloween/Christmas holiday season, nothing quickened the beat of my seven-year-old heart quite like the announcement of a field trip. We brought sand pails and pictures of oceanic creatures and went tidepooling at the seashore. We ate tuna sandwiches with cheddar cheese and apples. We identified seaweeds, crabs, sea stars, and hummed to periwinkles. On the ride home, we fell asleep.

We went to the Boston Museum of Science. We watched beavers build a lake in the Omni Theater and had a sleepover in the "wave room." We were scared of the life-sized model of T-Rex standing at the ready around the corner. It was awesome.

We went to the aquarium and saw parrot fish and tiger sharks, which also deliciously scared us. We watched penguins go down slides. On the ride home, of course, we fell asleep.

We played so hard and learned so much as kids that we had to sleep it off on the ride home. Play hard and rest hard is a great lesson to learn young. The field trip model is perfect for staycationing. When modeling your outings on the spirit of primary school, remember that a field trip must be:

1) Outside a classroom (office, mundane, etc.) setting

2) Mind-blowing (i.e. educational in a way you actually absorb).

Be honest: When was the last time you went to a museum? My fiance and I went to a post office museum on Prince Edward Island and saw a surprising and beautiful collection of *Anne of Green Gables*-era kitchen set-ups. The old post office was replete with feathery-handwritten script letters and old mail-carrier logs, but the museum's *piece de resistance* was a "mustache-friendly" teacup, which ensured a man's upper-lip coif would remain dry. (See Rule #2.)

A day spent at the museum is never better than at the end eating a sandwich on the marble steps. Remember that? Have yourself a cold juice-box, a salami and cheese, and a clutch of grapes with prime views of pigeons on statues.

If you really want to geek-out, do a little research before you go and have a scavenger hunt for your children/grandchildren/friends that never grew up. Print up lists, have stickers. You'll all flip—in a good way.

Some Museum Resources:
Abbe Museum - www.abbemuseum.org
Center for Maine Contemporary Art - www.artsmaine.org
Children's Museum of Maine - www.childrensmuseumofme.org
The Farnsworth - www.farnsworthmuseum.org
Owl's Head Transportation Museum - www.ohtm.org
Maine Discovery Museum - www.mainediscoverymuseum.org
Maine Historical Museum - www.mainehistory.org
Maine Maritime Museum - www.bathmaine.com
Maine State Museum - mainestatemuseum.org
Ogunquit Museum of American Art - www.ogunquitmuseum.org
Portland Museum of Art - www.portlandmuseum.org

Slow Down Time

Field trips (fulfilling their two awesome rules) are also a response to our "mind blowing" relationship to time, and why sometimes we feel present and sometimes we, quite literally, "go through the motions," without taking in much experience.

How we perceive time was addressed in an NPR piece a while back, and recently written about in *The New Yorker* by Burkhard Bilger about the studies of David Eagleman (April 25, 2011. p 54-65). The reporter in the radio show tested random people walking on the street with a simple test: for one half of the test, they stopped obviously young people (teens to early twenties) and for the other half of the test, they stopped obviously older people (eighties to nineties). They asked both groups when they thought a minute had passed. The younger group stopped around sixty seconds. The older group? Ninety seconds! Although they thought only a minute had passed, it was a minute and a half. This is because the world seems to move much faster for the older group.

Before you let this bum you out, let me fill you in on the reason behind it. Your mind is constantly documenting information that it feels is relevant or interesting. The first birthday you remember was so incredible because your mind took meticulous notes, documenting every smell, every color and conversation. The next year, and the years after, your mind recognized that birthday as being linked to the ones before, so its notes could be a bit more abridged. This is why we can find our way around our bedrooms in the dark: our minds have a picture, already, of the layout, and even when we're mostly asleep and have to pee, we don't trip over our nightstands. Our minds have already taken notes on it, and we don't need all of our senses to be present.

Apply this to your vacation and you understand why, when we travel or go to places we haven't been before, a week can seem like a month, a day like three days. Our minds are actually functioning at a higher level.

That's why walking to work a different way, taking ourselves on wild adventures, and spinning our lives in different directions is so important. It gives our hungry minds what they want! Your mind wants to be the A student, taking notes on every fascinating detail. It doesn't want to be taught the ABC's for the five hundredth time, so to speak. Cooking different things and reading different things and talking to different people and walking into different shops, coffee bars, and pubs are all ways to confuse your mind enough to spark the scribbling of thought that makes you feel alive and tells your brain "Ah, I'll need to look back on this later! I should *really* be writing this down!"

Do you need a more wonderful reason to learn?

Go on a True Adventure of Exaggerated Importance

Keeping in line with the trickery that is so helpful to keep your brain interested is the idea of the adventure, the quest, the journey, the exotic. *Exotic* is still a real thing—the definition of something being from far away, or rare—but it's lost much of its distinction. I don't think it can compare to what *exotic* meant to a prairie family eating an orange, for example. We appreciate the *exotic* because it is often hard to get, unattainable locally, and therefore usually expensive.

Luckily, this same feeling can happen without cost. It's called a Secret Squirrel Mission. A friend of mine introduced me to the phrase fifteen years back, and it's stuck. When I was a teenager, I would walk with a friend for five miles to get to a run-down antiques store – we were on a search for a vintage lunch box, I think. Though we came up empty-handed for the lunch box, we came across a roadside general store that sold mediocre steak and cheese subs – conquest! It was the mission that felt fun, and we had some riches to take back in our stomachs.

Another friend conjured up a Secret Squirrel Mission in search of abandoned apple orchards around Mount Desert Island. We found them through overgrown trails and forlorn foggy meadows. We went home, brewed fresh coffee, and made a buttery crisp with our plunder.

Things taste better and feel better when you have some idea of what went into getting them. Since this is a game, it's not even that important if the quest matches the win; I didn't slaughter my own cow to get a steak and cheese sandwich. It's the impish quality and a playful bit of theatrics that keep the goal in mind. Don't let luxury imprison you. Imagine up a journey and just pretend it's important.

Take the Ferry

A few years ago, I went to one of the Big Read's book discussions on Peaks Island. Peaks is an urban-safe oasis of a town next to Portland and a staycation destination—if there ever was one—but what I really learned from this event was this: Boats are awesome. For island people, this is no news, but for those of us who have somehow forgotten, listen up.

On a ferry to another island, I have:

1) Gotten pleasantly drunk on an Allagash Tripel while watching the sunset over Portland.
2) Seen a seal swim alongside the boat and poke its nose into the November sea spray.
3) Had the man of my dreams ask me to marry him.

And that was all before I got to the island!

If you're one of the folks of Maine who live near the big salty blue, get yourself a ferry schedule and keep it near your keys, in your car, in your rucksack. Think about taking the Mail Boat, a smaller, subtler option, that goes to all the islands for cheap. Maine's two thousand islands are incredibly diverse, ranging from isolated blips to summer art colonies to year-round townships with shops, restaurants, and schools. Some have lovely B&Bs, hotels, or camping options—if island exploration sounds like something you'd like to do for a few days. You could Secret Squirrel for old bikes to ride or try to find an island that makes its own beer (they're out there!).

Ferry Resources:

For Peaks Island and other islands in Casco Bay go to: www.cascobaylines.com

For Islesboro, Vinalhaven, North Haven, and Matinicus go to:

www.maine.gov/mdot/msfs

For Monhegan Island got to: www.balmydayscruises.com

Walk for Art

If you'd like to do something out of the ordinary and don't have a lot of cash, keep your eyes open for Maine Art Walks. Most larger towns and cities have regular art walks, often on the first Friday of the month. Museums, galleries, and shops are open late on these evenings, and often offer free wine and unusually festive conversation (see the free wine). Maine's art scene and its subsequent unified monthly hospitality help breathe life into the old fishing/industrial/mill cities and villages that have busted out with creative cuisine and art in recent decades. There is a necklace of small towns and cities strung along Route 1: Portland, Brunswick, Bath, Rockland, Belfast, and beyond - and they all have unique personalities. The festivals, evenings, and walks in these revitalized places cater to your need to get out and enjoy free entertainment and the open air. Chambers of commerce are a good place to start, when you're nosing around. (For a listing of art walks around the state: maineartscommission.blogspot. com/2010/11/explore-maines-artwalks.html)

Beach Pass

More open-air deals abound for us thrifty Yankees! If you like beaches (and if you don't, I feel sorry for you, I really do) get a state park pass. If you're planning ahead, you can check a box on your state tax return and get your pass in the mail, but you can also buy one at any state park, anytime. This takes so much stress out of going to the beach because you can just go whenever the mood hits. You don't have to worry about wasting money on the instantaneous development of an electrical storm or a twenty-degree drop in temperature. Your wallet needn't empty because Mother Nature has a sudden change of heart. You also don't have to stress if you can't completely fill your minivan with contributing beachgoers in order to soften the blow of the sometimes-steep beach fees. All real Mainers buy in bulk, anyway. (www.maine.gov/doc/parks/programs/parkpasses.html)

Picnic!

Who says you have to wait till lunch for a good picnic? Why not take your dog on a morning walk with the whole gang, stop in at the bakery for the fresh goodies, and go out for a morning picnic at the beach. Imagine a buttery croissant in your hand while your feet are washed by hypnotizing waves....

Or use the morning to think artisanal and make a basket of luscious, colorful, tender, flaky, juicy treats that you want to eat on your afternoon picnic. Don't bother with crinkly-packaged granola bars. Stay away from anything boring. Make a pressed sandwich and get fizzy fruit drinks in pretty bottles.

Or wait a few more hours and pack a cooler with your favorite marinated meats or some old-school franks and patties, and use one of those grills in the park. Bring fabric napkins and a Frisbee so you know it's special. Play checkers with rocks and a board drawn in the sand. Bring the guitar. Have a sing-along. The miles of coast are waiting.

Recipe: Pressed Sandwiches

These are made the day/a few hours before you'd like to enjoy them. They're great for picnics because "pressed" means the sandwiches hold together beautifully.
Serves 8

1 jar (12 oz.) oil-packed roasted red peppers (or fresh roast them yourself)
1 lb. fresh mozzarella, sliced thin
12 oz. thin-sliced salami
3/4 c fresh pesto
olives, pitted and torn, or olive spread
2 bunches arugula (6 oz. each, with thick stems removed)
olive oil (for brushing bread if using fresh roasted red peppers)
2 loaves ciabatta bread, cut lengthwise
salt and pepper to taste

Brush oil on the tender side of the sliced loaves. Sprinkle salt and pepper. Dividing evenly, layer bottom bread halves with the olives/olive spread, red peppers, mozzarella, salami, pesto, and arugula. Top with remaining bread halves. Wrap each sandwich tightly with wax paper or plastic, and press by laying wrapped sandwiches on a baking sheet, positioning another baking sheet on top, and weighting with a skillet or heavy canned goods. Let stand for one hour, pressing down occasionally with hands. Refrigerate wrapped sandwiches until ready to serve, up to 1 day. To serve, cut into wedges.

Pick-Your-Own Pastoral Afternoon

You're outside, you can eat as you go—it's pick-your-own! From spring strawberries and summer blueberries to fall apples and winter Christmas trees, Maine farms offer something to pick year round. Check GetRealMaine.com or PickYourOwn.org for the details, then pack up the car, and get picking. Bring your camera; you can finish your holiday greeting card photo on this outing, for sure.

Seasonally Speaking...Seasonally Seeking

The seasons are there for us to appreciate all of their personalities. A seventy-two-degree summer day wouldn't feel so luxurious if we didn't have a crisp, snow-show afternoon to compare it to. New England is an education in appreciation. Skating, leaf-peeping, boogie-boarding, hiking: all of these activities are free for the taking. Free stuff sometimes takes an initial small investment: ice skates, sleds, boogie boards, sand pails, and maybe big plastic bins for handy snow-fort construction —but you can get most of those for next to nothing at thrift stores. Maine is in the fortunate position of overflowing with a nostalgic general public that can support many second-hand stores. Now you just need a closet to stash them in—or plan to rent them and avoid the investment and storage issues all together.

Some Seasonal Resources:

Winter - www.visitmaine.com/attractions/winter_activities

Summer - www.visitmaine.com/attractions/outdoor_recreation_sports_adventure

---

Playground Tour

Hit as many playgrounds as you can in one day. Make your own guide and award different parks for best swing, best slide, best view, best sandbox, etc. Don't know where to start? Ask the first person who wanders by with a stroller, and go from there. (Note: You don't have to have kids to do this one!) (raisingmaine.mainetoday. com/playgrounds.html)

Swimming Hole Tour

Spend the day—or your whole staycation—touring local swimming holes. Make your own aquatic guide, noting the best caves, best jumps (check before you jump off ANYTHING!), best waterfalls, etc., for a great souvenir. Please note water levels before you swim in any river; still waters run *fast* sometimes! (www. swimmingholes.org/me.html)

Field Day

Remember Field Day? Tug-of-war, water balloon toss, fifty-yard-dash? Do it. Creating your own version of this school tradition is especially nice for family groups and friends from out of town. Remember to get award ribbons, serve up some orange slices, and let the games begin. (And I bet you could get everything you need at your nearest Reny's: www.renys.com)

Doggy Day Out

Remember when you first got Fido? How you went everywhere together and wouldn't consider a beach where dogs couldn't frolic off-leash? Make this a staycation for your furry friend, too, and spend a day pampering your pooch. Hit all the pet-friendly beaches, parks, and treat spots, and remember to sneak a little of your burger or ice cream cone to your buddy. (Note: Your neighbor's latch-key dog would be more than happy to help out if you don't have a dog of your own!)

Laugh at the Clouds

When it's warm, rain is welcome refreshment. Don't miss out! Put your kids and yourself into bathing suits and go out to play in the puddles. Hiking in the rain is beautiful. The water brings out smells that you don't get in the heat, and it's more refreshing than central air—as long as you don't mind hiking damp!

One of my best summer memories is of a rain shower at a friend's camp. The motor boats hurried into their docks, and the people of the lake hunkered down to put in a movie, but my adventurous relatives said, "Put on your bathing suits!" They strapped lifejackets onto my sisters and me, and we headed out onto the empty lake as raindrops fell around us. It was a secret place left just for us on the lake. No one else could appreciate that rain could be fun! We boogie-boarded for hours, my cousin dripping-wet and cackling, "They're all inside saying, "It's raining!"" (I'd like to think that it goes without saying that everyone should head inside at the first hint of thunder or lightning, but I'm saying it just in case. You don't want to test Mother Nature while enjoying your newfound love of inclement weather.)

Bonfires

If you light it, they will come. Invite your musical friends, your grill-queen, and your siren-voiced roommate to a bonfire evening. A bucket of beers, some sticks and hotdogs, and it's a party. Beach bonfires are my personal favorite, but not all Maine beaches allow them. Those that do usually require permits, so be sure to check local regulations and weather conditions.

Obstacle Courses

Not just for mini-golf anymore (although, that's still some good fun), there's a bunch of monkey-swinging adventures springing up around Maine. Whether they're modeled after summer-camp ropes courses or rock-climbing gyms, the professionals are there to help! Strap on the harness and feel the thrill of gravity.

Outdoor Movies

It's hard to go inside during our lovely summer, and luckily you don't have to—even if you want to see a movie. When the Saco Drive-in Theater opened in 1939, it was the first of its kind in Maine and only the second drive-in nationwide. Catch a movie and little bit of history there or at one of Maine's other remaining drive-ins.

Besides the drive-ins, there are many free options for outdoor movies during the warmer months. Bring a tote bag of popcorn and a bunch of Maine Root sodas (www.maineroot.com), get some paper straws, and sit under the stars on your nearest park lawn or parking garage.

Drive-Ins:
www.drive-ins.com/theaters/me/status_op=open

Saco Drive-In Theater:
969 Portland Road Route 1, Saco, ME 04072, 207- 284-1016

Pride's Corner Drive-In Theater:
651 Bridgton Road, Westbrook, ME 04092-3701, 207- 797-3154

Go a Huttin'

The beautiful Maine Huts are up and running. "Hut" isn't descriptive enough for these beautiful "walk-in only" lodges. With wooden interiors, fireplaces, and cozy reading nooks, they're an L.L. Bean dream. Some are by the water, and all bunk-houses smell like fresh-milled pine. At less than $100 a night (delicious meals included), this is a great low-impact way to spend the night in the woods. (Check mainehuts.org for more information.)

Asana in the Sun

Outdoor yoga classes are all over the state—at Acadia National Park, in Audubon centers, in public parks, and in instructors' own backyards. Most classes tend to pop up seasonally, so check local listings. Wherever you end up, chirping birds and a good morning stretch will set you straight.

Camp in Your Backyard

Get all the perks of camping (sounds of the outdoors, smells of grass, bird awakening) and the perks of running water and flushable toilets. Wear flannel shirts, light a fire, sing camp songs, toast ten marshmallows at once, roast a hot dog.

CHAPTER 4

Indoor Activities

I f you're having a staycation in a warmer month, great! You've got the obvious inspirations of lovely weather and warmth on your side for a "do anything" mindset. For cold weather months and rainy, often muggy days, an open mind and creative spirit is a must. It can certainly feel like the fates are conspiring when you have to be indoors because of winter freeze or cold rain—the grumpy threat of cabin fever lurking in the corner. But don't lose heart! There are plenty of wonderful things to experience when you have a few days inside. Meet the introverted sister of outside play: indoor activities.

Mid-day Light

I remember relishing the thought of staying home sick from school. I would swallow really hard and make sure that I didn't feel any soreness, make sure the sweat from my down-blanket insulation wasn't a fever. The slightest hint of "feeling off" would have me looking for my ticket out of school for the day. FREEDOM! I would spend the day watching cinema classics like *Hairspray* and *Dirty Dancing* and drinking pink ginger ale in my parents' bed. Those days were spectacular. I had them all to myself, with no agenda, and I got the experience of seeing my house in the mid-day light. There is something about stumbling into a different time of day in a familiar environment. Anyone who has opened a bar at 1PM could tell you that. It feels like an empty stage. The anticipation and freedom of dwelling in such a charged place is thrilling. You feel like you're doing something forbidden, or like you have the inside scoop on an intimate personal surrounding.

As a kid, some of the sick-day thrill came from watching as much television as I wanted; "it makes you a zombie!" was a favorite chant of my mother. But more important was the thrill of doing something my friends at school weren't doing; of getting out of the rules for a day. There was no one there to see me, so I'd often dress-up, just because my mother's gowns from the Seventies seemed right while sipping on lemon with honey in it. I didn't have anyone's eyebrows raised in my direction and I could pursue my own happiness, even if it came with the price of flu-like symptoms.

Vacations, of course, don't need to be driven with a sick day. But use that as an excuse to the world if it's what gets you liberated to see the shorter shadows in your living room.

Make the Indoors Last

Getting inspired while inside is one thing; staying that way is another! Beware of lazy distractions while cozying in at home. Idle preoccupation is the vacation sieve: don't let it happen to you! I'm not saying you can't indulge in a much-needed *Laverne & Shirley* marathon, but make sure it's what you want before it pulls you into its entertaining clutches. I'm not sure how many channels televisions have nowadays. The obscene number gets higher all the time, and each channel is geared more specifically to what kind of mood you're in, minute to minute. So before you spend your staycation ingesting 36 hours of Baywatch, History Channel mummy dissections, or Emeril saying "BAM!" every time he adds a tablespoon of garlic, think about your intentions. Make sure it's what you want to do and not just something that's *there*. Hours can pass in front of the tube, and you just don't want to waste them. It's like eating a cake while sleepwalking; you didn't even get to enjoy it, and now it's gone.

Candle-lit Everything

Staying present and making *staying in* a vacation has a lot to do with crackling fires. I mean: Hello, romance. Someone lighting a fire for you is in the same column as someone turning down your bed, running you a bath, or fixing you a stiff drink when the occasion calls for it. It's the feeling that you're being taken care of. A fireplace is ideal, but for those with metallic heat sources that hiss and creak from floorboards, I strongly recommend enthusiastic candle use.

A lot of people don't realize how much mood is affected by the flickering, dynamic light and heat of candles and fireplaces. I mean, of course, we know it's romantic and that the lighting is good on complexions. But there is something about flipping on the overhead kitchen fluorescent that says "party's over." Since it's your party, you're the one that has to clean up and turn on the lights of reality – or choose to keep them dim and tell your festivity-starved spirit that it's still time to play, even while washing dishes.

So stoke the fire or light the candles and rewrite your notion of romance. It doesn't have to mean sexy romance—although that's very nice—but what my family used to call "Ambiance Time." There would be music, a solid wedge of Jarlsberg with crackers, wine for my mother and a hoppy beer for my father, and we would make pizzas together. It was lovely, and special, and infinitely more memorable than ordering take-out. Ambiance time isn't the most efficient way to make dinner, but as a very dear friend of mine once wisely told her husband, "Sweetheart, the point of romantic things is that they aren't practical, convenient, or logical. You leave romantic notes for me to find and get rare LPs of the Bangles for me because it's romantic, not because you can write it off on your taxes."

Dance Party

Spontaneous dance parties can occur at the one-two punch of a string of Christmas lights and the drop of a bass beat. Headlamps work in a pinch, if you're outdoorsy. You can spend weeks creating the perfect playlist or just hit shuffle on your iPod. The point is to crank some tunes and show off your moves.

Blanket Forts

Kids love forts and hidden spaces away from parties. How about a party in a blanket fort? Get your biggest blankets out (remember those crappy lap-throws falling in and ruining your shelter?) and bring body pillows and couch cushions out for yourselves and your kids. You'll want to crawl in and play along.

Board Games

How many board games are stacked in your closet right now? How long has it been since you played them? It's time to break them out and give them a twist. Mix up the pieces, make up new rules, use three different boards at once – just *play.*

Cooking Projects

Get the imported Irish butter for herb popcorn. Get the really good chocolate. Don't hold back on quality; it's not the time.

Some of My Favorite Sites When I Need Inspiration

Mad Hungry *with Lucinda Scala Quinn: She specializes in easy-going family-style, simple comfort food with nutrition in mind. (blog.madhungry.com)*

Gluten Free Girl and the Chef: *It's not just lame substitutions. This is real cuisine and she's fun to read. (glutenfreegirl.com)*

Jamie Oliver: *I think you've heard of the guy. His style is fun, approachable, and the "food porn" is amazing. (www.jamieoliver.com)*

Craft Projects

Get out the fabric scraps and make those doll clothes you and your kid have been talking about for months. I mean, how much longer is she going to be in the second grade? Make matching pajama pants for the whole family or spend the afternoon fingerpainting – it doesn't really matter. This is about sitting down with each other and making something. If you want to tackle something big, or something tricky, the blogosphere is full of experts with beautiful photo tutorials of crafting, cooking, and home-fixer-upping. If you want to stick with the basics and break out a new box of Crayolas, that's okay, too.

Some Favorite Sites When You Need Inspiration

SouleMama (www.soulemama.com)
Purl Bee (www.purlbee.com)
Spool (www.spoolsewing.com)
Martha Stewart Living *(www.marthastewart.com/crafts)*

Make Your Own Playdough

It's so easy to make. This is a cooked variety, because the texture is great. But if you'd prefer to make it with your kids, there is an uncooked version below.

Cooked Playdough

2 cups flour
2 cups warm water
1 cup salt
2 tablespoons vegetable oil
1 tablespoon cream of tartar (optional for improved elasticity)
Food coloring (optional)
Scented oils (optional)

Mix all the ingredients and stir over very low heat. The dough will begin to thicken until it resembles mashed potatoes. When the dough pulls away from the sides and clumps in the center, remove the pan from heat and allow the dough to cool enough to handle. If your playdough is still too sticky, just cook it a bit longer.

Uncooked Playdough

1/2 cup salt
1/2 cup water
1 cup flour
Food coloring (optional)

Mix ingredients together and knead in food coloring as final step!
PS: When using food coloring, be careful of your counters! Put down newspaper or something when you're all playing around with dyed dough on pale counter tops!

Movie Marathon

Set a theme. Say, for example, you'd like to watch the original *The Parent Trap*: make an Italian dinner, stick some candles into old wine bottles, and put a checkered blanket on the TV-room floor. Or play camp counselors with your family and friends in the yard and watch the movie at the end of the day. You can whistle the marching theme as you march around your kitchen island. Use any movie to create any theme you'd like.

DIY Spa Day

Cucumbers on the eyes, white towel in the hair. Get buckets and give yourself/each other pedicures. Do silly fun stuff. Draw yourself a bath. Put on your Enya-esq music. Hire a massage therapist to come to your house—if you've got some of that money saved up! Let the lavender therapy begin!

Fashion Show

All those things you're saving for a special occasion? This is it! Break out your highest heels, your sleekest chic, and your blingiest bling, and strut your stuff. Let the kids dress up in your good stuff, and let them dress you up, too!

Georgia O'Keeffe Night

Painting is fun, especially when you have a few tools under your belt to help your creative visions along. Watercolor paper really does make a difference, and so do nice brushes and paint – but that doesn't mean you can't have fun with copy paper and those old-school watercolor six-packs from Crayola. Add a little masking tape for fancy frames and collect a few crayons—they keep paint pigment off and let you do really cool effects.

Once your supplies are ready, set up a still life and paint a quiet morning away. Put a permanent pot of Earl Grey and milk out and sip, sip, sip as you brush and blend. Put on some majestic symphony music, like Handel's *Water Music*, Vivaldi's *The Four Seasons*, or Bach's Brandenburg concertos, and pretend you're an Edwardian noblewoman. Or cultivate the starving artist thing and replace the tea with a bottle of red wine. (Looking for some artistic tips? Try www.watercolorpainting.com)

Stitch

If you have a sewing machine, you know how meditative an afternoon as a seamstress can be. Even if you don't, some needles and thread and one of many adorable (and available for free online) stuffed animal patterns might be your ticket to a quiet afternoon.

You can't beat Jo-Ann Fabrics for one-stop shopping and a crazy assortment of textiles, but visiting your local fabric store is way more staycation-minded—and way more fun. There will be fewer fabric choices, for sure, but the quality of the fabric and the experience will be far superior—and you're likely to meet some delightful crafters who are more than happy to help you along.

(If you need some on-line hand-holding, try whipping up this lovely little fabric bird. It can be a toy or an ornament, and the pattern is free here: www.spoolsewing. com/blog/wp-content/uploads/2008/06/birdpattern1-1.pdf

Get Cooking

I'm going to say this again: Go into the kitchen. Make something. Anything. Sometimes the simplest thing – like stovetop popcorn when you've forgotten it comes out of anything but the microwave – can be as rewarding as a four-course meal. Go. Cook.

Stovetop Popcorn
Once you make this simple snack, you'll be aghast that you haven't made it for the past ten movie nights. It's cheap and you'll empty a five-gallon bowl, no problem.
Makes 1, I mean, 6 servings.

> 2–3 T oil
> $2/3$ c popcorn
> Butter
> Herbs (optional)
> Heavy bottom med/large size pan with a lid

Pour oil in pan and set to med/high heat. Add 3-4 kernels of popcorn and fit the lid on tightly. Wait for the kernels to pop (you'll hear it) and add the rest of the popcorn. Put the lid on tightly again and shake to distribute the oil evenly. Shake every few seconds to make sure the popcorn isn't burning on the bottom. Listen for when the popping has almost entirely stopped and remove from heat. Pour into a big bowl. In the pan that's still hot, but not on a burner, put in the amount of butter you'd like (3-4 T is a good place to start), and let it melt in the pan. If you'd like herbs, add approx. half tsp to the butter to awaken the herb. Pour onto popcorn and toss.

If you just ate popcorn for dinner, you're going to need some dessert!

This is the best chocolate cake I've ever had. Make sure you have at least a half-gallon of milk waiting in the fridge to accompany perfection.

Chocolate Cake
Makes a double layer cake, 10-12 servings

2 cups sugar
1¾ cups all-purpose flour
¾ cup dutch/any cocoa
1½ teaspoons baking powder
1½ teaspoons baking soda
1 teaspoon salt
2 eggs
1 cup milk
½ cup vegetable oil
2 teaspoons vanilla extract
1 cup boiling water (it sounds weird, but, believe me, it makes a
  difference)
chocolate frosting (recipe to follow)

I. Heat oven to 350°F. Grease and flour (with cocoa) two 9-inch round baking pans.

2. Stir together sugar, flour, cocoa, baking powder, baking soda, and salt in large bowl. Beat in eggs, milk, oil, and vanilla on medium speed until smooth. Stir in boiling water (batter will be thin). Pour batter into pans.

3. Bake 30 to 35 minutes or until wooden pick inserted in center comes out clean. Cool 10 minutes; remove from pans to wire racks. Cool completely. Frost with frosting of your choice. I recommend going all-out and making this:

Chocolate Frosting

$1/2$ cup (1 stick) butter
$2/3$ cup cocoa
3 cups powdered sugar
$1/3$ cup milk
1 teaspoon vanilla extract

Melt butter. Stir in cocoa. Alternately, add powdered sugar and milk, beating to spreading consistency. Add a little bit more milk, if needed. Stir in vanilla.

Party

This can be a great thing at the beginning or end of your staycation. I'm not sure if you're going to have a whole week or a long weekend to staycation, but having a party can be great. Some people love throwing a party and some hate it. You could always have a casual event at a location, like a beach or a pub, if cleanup says "all work and no play" to you.

Clam and Lobsterbakes are a coveted no-brainer choice for warm-month gatherings. Ice skating and sledding take care of cold festivities, once you make hot cocoa!

Ghost Story Party

Not only for October (although it fits nicely), a good ghost story is certainly a big part of the New England tradition! With the lights turned low and devilish drinks in hand, spinning tales with a few brave (or squeamish—they're the most fun to scare!) friends turns your time together into Poe-proportions.

Sharing the Calm and Blissful Atmosphere You've Created

You can also choose a peaceful route with a selective approach to company. Invite your quieter friends and loved ones to come sit around with you. They won't expect you to entertain them, and they know when to suggest a game of rummy.

If you do choose to invite friends along, just be sure they're game for the kind of relaxation you have in mind. To anyone that will draw you from your paradise: You're not home. You have to remind yourself of this. It's an important part of staycationing that is the only strong-willed thing you need to hold to the sticking place: Don't give your vacation time away.

CHAPTER 5

Going Out

We all hate to leave the comfort of a throw blanket and Ben & Jerry's when we've had a hard day, but going out is very, very good for you. I needn't tell you that the last good laugh you had was not while watching *Dynasty* with your loveable dachshund. (Um, was it?) Comb your hair, splash on the fancy aftershave or eau de toilette, and make a break for the door.

Now what?

Bite the bullet and get a ticket to a show you've really wanted to see. Think like you did as a kid, when those kinds of events were really special. I remember looking forward to concerts for months at a time. Allow yourself to geek out. Better yet, share in geeking out with a loved one. Listen to the latest record from your band-of-choice for days ahead of time. Play it loud, in your living room, with a cocktail or beer on the night of the show. Anticipate the stuff out of it.

When it comes to kids, I say it takes a village. Our children and close relatives can truly benefit from shared time together. Keep saying that over and over again to your family, friends, and children, and get your kids under someone else's watchful eye for a while. Some of the best days of my entire life were spent with babysitters. The babysitter jungle gym, the babysitter who fed me watermelon and brownies, the babysitter who made us little animals out of wool felt. For all the fun my parents built into my life, they couldn't compete with the novelty of an energetic babysitter. Stop feeling guilty and remember that your kids look forward to a good babysitter at least as much as you do!

Your staycation could be the perfect time to test the waters with the trustworthy cousin you've got in NYC who wants to take care of your kids for the weekend, or ship them off to Grampy's house for some ice fishing. That means you can do what you want and they get an experience. Trust the universe with your children. It takes a village for you to relax.

A Tourist for a Day

There's no gloom that white knee socks and a Hawaiian shirt can't fix. It might be embarrassing, but go see what all the fuss is about. Support your neighbor who pulls the wool over the eyes of out-of-towners each summer and go on a duckboat ride and see buildings you walk by each day through the eyes of someone from Yonkers. Go get a shirt with a lobster on it.

Be a tourist for a day somewhere you almost think is lame, but not quite. Some of these activities offer discounts for locals, so ask before you jump in as a complete "from awayer."

Being a tourist for a day is ballsy and takes some acting ability. The thing that makes tourists "tourists" is their complete cluelessness about their ignorance. I mean that warmly; they're just enjoying themselves.

But it's that benign grin—that trust in suggestions that come from a leaflet at the train station or hotel—that makes tourists like children, depending on others for knowledge, advice, and how not to get stuck somewhere when the tide comes in. Most of us have been tourists at one point or another. Maybe we didn't want to admit it, but we were there, maps spread out for all locals to see like an open trenchcoat.

Giving in to that innocence can open doors of appreciation in your adventure-hungry heart. Try on someone else's hat. Go on a lighthouse tour. Go see about the Maine Huts. Wander into a clam-digging field even if—*especially if*—mollusks kind of creep you out.

Get a goofy hat. Ask the waiter questions you know the answer to and see what kind of responses you get. See if you get them believing and see if they suggest clam chowder and lobster, like you know they will. See if they suggest blueberry pie for dessert when you say you really want the "Maine experience." Try to ask for everything authentic. You're a child of Maine. Let yourself act like one.

Museums

There are so many: art, history, science, firestation, cryptozoology. You name it. The architecture alone should be enough to get you out of the house. (See *page 40* for some museum resources.)

Shows

Whether you have a top-secret thing for the Josh Groban-esque or you would love to see a murder-mystery play while you eat a pizza, the options in Maine (especially during summer stock season) are endless. There are so many old theaters in the Pine Tree State. The second that smell of aged varnish hits your nose, you know something dramatic is going to happen. Put on something that goes along with the plot, and really soak it up.

On the musical side of things, there are riotous Celtic jams, and rock bands that will make you (but not your morning-after-thrash neck) feel fifteen again. There are salsa classes that teach you as a live band plays into the late hours. There are national acts that want to come to Maine and arena shows, as well as intimate and better-ventilated clubs that can bring you within the close orbit of fame. (For theater and venue listings: www.visitmaine.com/attractions/arts_and_entertainment/performing_arts/theater)

Book Signings

Maine has its share of famous writers, from Stephen King and Richard Russo to Tess Gerritsen and Julia Spencer-Fleming—and there's a lot you haven't heard of yet. In an age when big-box bookstores have crowded out the local competition in much of the country, Maine still boasts a number of intimate, cozy local bookstores. Readings often include cheese, wine, and other refreshments, and always feature interesting conversation. They are just as fabulous as you imagine. And you can usually get the author to write something cheeky inside the cover.

Plan Your Foodie Staycation

You're going to pack in some caloric miles here, so map out your tastebuds' adventure accordingly. Go to the *best* restaurants you've overheard about over morning coffee or your best friend has implored you to try. Go with a willing partner in crime, or if your kids are older and you don't think your tasting dollars will be wasted on whiners who would rather have plain noodles with butter, bring them along! Epicurean exploration will make you feel like you're part of an upper tax bracket, and you don't have to leave the state. I went to Paris to visit a friend recently. Believe me. They have nothing on Maine cuisine.

Café Board Games

This is even more fun if you don't have the game yet. Go to a toy store on the way to a café you either already adore or you haven't tried yet (grown-ups, this also works with certain cozy pubs). Get one of many board games that has surged in popularity in recent years like Settlers of Catan, The Rivals for Catan, or Dominion—or grab a deck of cards and go classic. There are wonderful rule guidelines now available online, so if you're like me and can't keep your gin straight from your cribbage, use a friendly Web informant. You can pass happy hours sipping on fine, foamy drinks and nibbling on café fare whilst you win over landmasses and defeat your daughter's army. Your imagination hasn't had this much fun in a long time.

Bachelor(ette)-Like Night

Dress up with your best friends and go *out*. List some crazy things for you to complete within your innocent town (asking silly questions to strangers, singing a lame song sincerely to a stranger, kissing a bald man on the head...we've all been there). It's a lot like your last night as a single person without the nearby lurking presence of inlaws. Boogie. Drink. Make a (jolly) scene!

Go on a Talk

There are talented speakers that offer (often free) live lectures in places all over the state. Make it your business to learn something more that you'd like to explore!

Check your local library – it probably has a lecture series, and your librarian definitely knows where to send you if it doesn't.

(To find information on a Maine library near you: www.maine.gov/msl)

Comfort Food Tour

Throughout one day of your staycation (or throughout the week, if you're so inclined!) go on a taste-testing tour to compare your favorite food at several eateries. Try eggs benedict three ways, four different bacon cheeseburgers, or chocolate cake at several butter-and-sugar establishments. Or, to put a different spin on it, leave the comparisons at the door and just eat all of your favorite comfort foods! Mac and cheese for brunch, lasagna at noon, and sausage and onion pizza for dinner! Now that sounds like vacation. Eat like a fourteen-year old on a growth spurt, have Tums at the ready, and take a day-after spa retreat to recover.

Brunch, Brunch, Brunch.

It's so much more festive than its adjacent meals and there are more hours of sleep built into the very meaning of it. You can get an entire carafe of coffee and bagels, and ask your buddies to bring the mimosa supplies. A little lox, and now you're fancy. Pick up copies of the *Times*, magazines, and have a card-making table around Valentine's Day or Christmas. Sit around and chat, play celebrity. Have a party that hardly costs anything, and cleanup goes in the recycle bin. You can spend the time you would on cleanup looking for movie times when you all decide to score a matinee.

CHAPTER 6

A Professional Staycationer

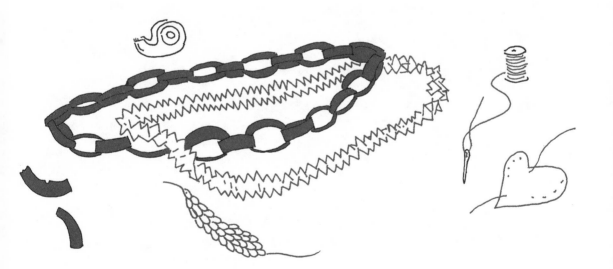

Certain people seem to be born with an innate ability to staycation. They're often the same annoyingly well-adjusted people who remember their discount coupons to concerts and call ahead for the 7P.M. restaurant reservation. We can learn from these friends. Fake it until we make it.

My friend, Michelle Souliere, is one of these people. She's written a phenomenal Secret Squirreling book, *Strange Maine: True Tales from the Pine Tree State*, based almost entirely on whimsical and sometimes creepy field trips she takes across this fascinating, balsam-fragrant state. She packs a sandwich, brings a friend and has a destination in mind. She gets there, pokes around, asks questions, and comes back home richer in the knowledge of the world around her.

Since Michelle is the closest person I've found to a professional staycationer, I asked her a few questions, and she was kind enough to share some secrets.

Why do you think you get off your butt and go out into the world on little and bigger local adventures more than the average Joe?

I've always thought being bored is your own fault. Also, I'm incorrigibly curious. And reading, while good and entertaining and informative, is never the same as going out and experiencing something —it's just common sense!

What do you recommend to someone who would like to staycation more, or adventure more, and how to prioritize it?

The next time you drive past something that looks interesting, remember it, and go back and actually visit later when you have time. The same goes for places that you hear about. Make yourself a little list of destination points. Then when you have a little gap in your schedule and you want to do something fun or different, grab that list and make some quick plans! Really, you've got nothing to lose.

How do you organize, remember, and prioritize your outings? Do you keep a list, have a good memory, put a color-coded chart on your fridge? What?

I take photos, and always grab a brochure or business card while I'm there. The photos are key—if I see something interesting that I want to know more about later, be it an item or a placard, I make sure to document it so later I can do some more poking around on my own at home or at the library. And carrying the brochure around with me guarantees I have a handy place to make notes for later info, which I won't lose because the notes and brochure will all be in one place!

Do you go solo a lot or usually take along a friend or your husband?

I find outings are more fun with a friend, especially if you have a friend who is either a) as rabidly curious as yourself or b) easygoing and ready to do whatever you want to do because they just like hanging out with you (and vice versa). Sometimes it's great to go alone, but I often find myself wishing there was someone with me to exclaim over particularly wacky or stunningly beautiful moments and views. Either way, these outings are a great way to get to know more about yourself and/or a friend via new adventures.

What makes a trip more fun? Which ones do you enjoy best, do you think, and why?

A certain amount of spontaneity is essential. In other words, don't research your outing to death! Just establish the basic details (hours, directions, cost) and go.

It also helps to allow good time cushions on either side of your destination for unplanned puttering about, gawking, dawdling, and a bite to eat, whether at a local diner or café, or in the form of a picnic lunch. Don't be afraid to navigate off the beaten path if you spot something that looks interesting or appealing.

Honestly, I enjoy them all. There's always something new to look at, because you're going somewhere you've never really explored. Paying attention to detail instead of engaging in nothing but cursory glances also ensures success. Why prepare to be bored when you could be fascinated?

Do you have a favorite type of adventure? Outside? Historic? Wilderness?

I like 'em all, but tend to plan outdoor stuff for the warmer months and indoor museums and such for the colder months. Some attractions have seasonal hours, and may not be open outside of the May–October tourist season, so make sure to plan ahead.

What do you always take with you on an adventure?

Camera. Extra batteries. Pen. Water.

Where are good places to find ideas for adventures?

Local magazines, like *Down East, Yankee,* and *Portland Magazine.* If you're passing through a town elsewhere, grab some of the free publications they have at the rest stop!

What bio information should I include and your what's book's official title?

Michelle Souliere is the author of *Strange Maine: True Tales from the Pine Tree State* and editor of the *Strange Maine Gazette* and blog (www.strangemaine.blogspot.com). She spends her time running the Green Hand Bookshop in Portland, Maine, and tries to fit as many field trips as she can into her ludicrously crammed-tight schedule.

CHAPTER 7

Tips on Re-Entry

Tips on Re-entry

How you talk about your staycation is an important part of it. People are going to want to know about it and how they can do it. There will also be those creeps who went to Prague or the Caribbean, and they might be inclined to diminish what you just had, saying that you "just stayed home." First off: Don't listen to them. You've made vacation a part of your life by introducing the concept to familiar surroundings. They have to come back to the same place they left, and if they're talking like that, I doubt they have the newfound appreciation for it that you do. You'll be more inclined to embrace a space as one to relax in, whereas they will be more inclined to think they need to be "elsewhere" to have a good time.

If you enjoy the documentary arts, a travel journal, photo album, or scrapbook can be a nice way to round out or ease out of your staycation. The organization will get you back on the Type A mindset that the rest of the world demands and you can take a nostalgic look at photos of all the cool stuff you just did. This part really helps make it feel real, as well, and will help reinforce that to your neighbors and coworkers when you go back. This doesn't seem like a huge deal, but people want proof, and sometimes that comes in the form of a picture of you jumping from a ledge into a sunlit swimming hole, or a photo-finish between you and your wife in a sledding race.

One-hour Vacations

One way to keep the feeling of staycation going on any old day is take a one-hour vacation. I went to 158—a wood-stove warmed Hobbit-hole of a breakfast bagel joint in South Portland that just so happens to be next to "Bug Light" lighthouse and a dog-friendly beach. In the hour that I could have been fumbling with online Web sites, dreaming of Icelandic architecture or Dutch linens, or watching kitty-dubbed You Tube videos, I had a catch-up with an old friend and shared in her creative ideas, got to eat roasted garlic with a fresh-and-chewy bagel, and took a walk on a beautiful breakwater overlooking Portland, Fort Gorges, and Peaks Island.

That hour is what I call a one-hour vacation. It seems like longer, in a very good way, and you feel refreshed in a way you couldn't after staring at a screen.

Staycation Every Day

There is a well-liked couple who come into my favorite coffee shop, Arabica, every day and they both order cappuccinos. They know everyone who sits at the bar, and they're always on their way to and from some place of productivity—two hard-working migratory birds in the city, perching down to rest. This is their ritual —their peaceful place - where they sip, chat, listen to music, hug friends, feel connected. I wonder when they started this—when they made it a priority. Nine out of ten times, they sit and stay. They don't "go!" with their coffee. They sit and rest. They had to start it some time.

Unusual, as well as cozy familiar things, make us feel good. We need the unusual to feel alive and we need the cozy familiar to feel recharged and rested. They are the two ingredients, really, for staycation success.

Screen-based entertainment has some wonderful visions to offer, but its proliferation has gotten the better of us. Interacting with the world makes us engaged, compassionate, fun people. Holding yourself accountable to your own experiences instead of sitting and watching someone else's is usually a life-changing choice. Be a good parent to yourself: turn off the TV and go outside! If you think of something that sounds interesting, go do it; write it down and put all the intention you can muster behind it.

If you intend to make your life better, livelier, lighter, put your feet behind it. You can make a decision to have fun; no one is stopping you. If they are, sneak this book to them on their office desk, under their pillow, in the mail. They could use a staycation!

There are so many reasons to go exploring off the well-worn paths of your life. Perhaps because you're looking for something cool to do this weekend, something a little different. Perhaps your children keep asking to pull over at the World's Biggest Blueberry road-stop, and you're finally ready to say, "Let's do it." You'll be their hero. Maybe you're ready to drive a different way home from work, and maybe that way will take you to watch the sunset over the water.

Where are you going on your next staycation?

Resource
Guide

Spas

Nine Stones, Portland
This Portland day spa is the perfect spot to ring in the new year with a fresh face to the world. Nine Stones offers an assortment of facials — from organic, pure-cleanse treatments to Dr. Hauschka-branded two-hour indulgences. Its Commercial Street location makes it a prime place to pair your hours of relaxation with lunch in the Old Port and some post-holiday sales shopping. *250 Commercial Street, Portland. 207-772-8480. www.ninestonesspa.com*

Kismet Inn, Bath
This charming, one-of-a-kind inn in the City of Ships offers a couples retreat weekend Feb. 11-13. The inn offers guided meditation and yoga, Thai Body Massage, a Signature Eastern Body Exfoliation, and more. Plus, dine on delicious, organic, and locally sourced food with an Iranian flair. *44 Summer Street, Bath. 207-443-3399. www.kismetinnmaine.com*

LilyPond Aquatic Therapies, Rockport
How does a late winter dunk in a saltwater pool sound? If it's at this aquatic therapy spa in Rockport, you'll find it to be ninety-seven degrees and rejuvenating. The spa, which offers a range of in-water options including Watsu, Aquatic Integration, and Water Dance, also has massage and energy treatments available. *120 Union Street, Rockport. 207-236-6616. www.lilypondaquatic.com*

The Portland Regency Hotel & Spa, Portland
Mud season in Maine can be a rather dreary time of year — unless, of course, that mud is wrapped around your body as part of a rejuvenating spa treatment. Treat yourself to a night at this Old Port hotel and try the Regency Signature Mineral Mud Wrap. You'll feel rested and refreshed without having to travel far. *20 Milk Street, Portland. 207-774-4200. www.theregency.com*

Soakology Foot Spa and Teahouse, Portland
No time like spring to spruce up your toes, since the sandals will be coming out of the closet soon (fingers crossed!). This Portland spa is almost entirely devoted to feet. Relax in a cushy sanctuary chair and allow your tootsies to be pampered in a warm cocoa mud wrap or a foot soak infused with lavender, seaweed, beach rose, or chocolate. *30 City Center, Portland. 207-879-7625. www.soakology.com*

White Barn Inn, Kennebunk
A weekend at this top-notch inn in Kennebunk is sure to be one of the most elegant getaways of your lifetime. Why not add a relaxing sea salt or milk bath and Swedish massage to make your trip even more memorable? Make sure the inn's food is part of your plan to indulge yourself. *37 Beach Avenue, Kennebunk. 207-967-2321. www.whitebarninn.com*

Fairwinds Spa, Sebasco

Nothing beats a July day at Popham Beach, except maybe a July morning at Popham Beach followed by an afternoon spent relaxing at this nearby resort spa. We recommend the Wild Beach Rose Hydrating Cocoon or the Sea Lavender Body Bliss. Even better: opt for an en suite massage. *Sebasco Harbor Resort, 29 Kenyon Road, Sebasco Estates. 207-389-1161 www.sebasco.com*

Cliff House, York

This renowned spa and resort a stone's throw from Ogunquit offers deep relaxation with an ocean view. Check out the "tapas treatments," abbreviated services to mix and match, such as the invigorating Blueberry and Rice Body Polish. Or try the spa sampler — three mini-treatments, a glass of wine, and hors d'oeuvres, available in the evenings on Thursdays and Sundays. *Shore Road, York. 207-361-1000. www. cliffhousemaine.com*

Bar Harbor Club, Bar Harbor

After a day hike in Acadia National Park, head to this historic spa for a De Stress Muscle Massage. Although the tennis, pool, fitness, and other activities are for club members only, the spa is open to the public. Envisioned by Nelson Rockefeller nearly four generations ago, the spa is housed in an iconic Tudor-style building constructed in the 1930s. *111 West Street, Bar Harbor. 207-288-5251. www.barharborclub.com*

Cottage Breeze Day Spa, Kennebunk

With the arrival of Columbus Day weekend comes a lovely sense of calm in the streets of Kennebunk and Kennebunkport, and without the hassles of traffic and tourists, a getaway to this summer haven is all the more relaxing. Save time to pop into this casual day spa for a soothing Maine River Stones Massage. *31 Western Avenue, Kennebunk. 207-967-2259. www.cottagebreeze.com*

Beauty Mark Spa, Camden

Just across the street from this seaside town's iconic library sits this spa in the beautifully renovated High Mountain Hall building. It's a great place to get one of several advanced skin-care treatments, such as the Microdermabrasion or Gentle Gel Peel. If you're in an active mood, schedule your spa treatment so you can drop in on one of High Mountain Hall's yoga classes, offered upstairs. *5 Mountain Street, Camden. 207-230-1170. www.beautymarkspa.com*

Inn by the Sea, Cape Elizabeth

Head to this oceanfront inn for an off-season retreat. You'll get a good deal on the room, which makes the ninety-minute signature Sea Waves Massage – a full body rub-down with aromatic oil and surround sound waves – an affordable holiday gift to yourself. *40 Bowery Beach Road, Cape Elizabeth. 207-799-3134. www. innbythesea.com*

Waterfalls

Abol Falls, on the West Branch of the Penobscot River, (T2 R10 WELS) features a gradual drop with road access.

Allagash Falls, on the Allagash River, (T15 R11 WELS) is a thundering cascade featuring a series of falls.

Angel Falls, on Mountain Brook, (Township D), is one of the highest drops in Maine, at thirty yards, even if such a cascade doesn't compare with its South American counterpart. This one's a little trickier to get to, though: follow the old railroad line off Route 17 in Houghton. Once you get to Berdeen Stream after a gravel pit, you'll have to ford the stream and then follow it along the north side until you reach the falls. The view will be worth it.

Bickford Slides, on Bickford Brook in Stow, is essentially two waterfalls, both fed by the same mountain stream. The water pours over an open ledge at the lower part of the falls, but the upper falls are even more spectacular. The good news is that both are accessible by offshoots of the White Mountain National Forest Bickford Brook Trail. Take **Blueberry Ridge** for the lower falls or the side path known as Bickford Slides Loop to reach the Upper Slides. Take care, however, because the crossing can be challenging at high water.

Big Niagara Falls, on Nesowadnehunk Stream (T3 R10 WELS), features a six-yard drop over stunning pink Katahdin granite.

The Cataracts, on Frye Brook in Andover West Surplus, offer another great opportunity for a waterfall visit. With three different scenic drops (from six- to nine-yards-high), this one is worth the trek. And if you're up for even more of a trek, the Appalachian Trail passes right by these falls.

Cold Stream Falls, on Cold Stream in Johnson Mountain Township, includes ruins around a small falls.

Debsconeag Falls, on the West Branch of the Penobscot River (T2 R10 WELS), features swift rapids on a well-known canoe route.

Dunn Falls, on the West Branch of the Ellis River in Andover North Surplus, includes a seventeen- and a twenty-six-yard drop on a spectacular mountain stream.

Earley Landing Falls, on Big Wilson Falls in Willimantic, includes some interesting geological features on a pair of two-yard drops.

The Falls, on Sandy Stream in Sandy Bay, features a dramatic drop in a bedrock cleavage.

Fish River Falls, on the Fish River (T14 R8 WELS), features fishing and camping near this dramatic canyon drop.

Grand Falls, on the Dead River (T3 R4 BKP WKR), includes an old dam near this horshoe falls, situated near the newest of Maine Huts & Trails' backcountry lodges.

Grand Falls, on Wassataquoik Stream (T4 R9 WELS), includes a series of falls with the bonus of having the remains of lumbering camps in the area.

Grand Pitch, on the East Branch of the Penobscot River (T5 R8 WELS), includes a stunning seven-yard drop.

Green Falls, on Wassataquoik Stream (T4 R10 WELS), sees the stream pass through a dramatic rock chute.

Hay Brook Falls, on Hay Brook in Bowdoin College Grant East, features three separate chutes.

Heald Stream Falls, on Heald Stream in Bald Mountain Township, includes a bridge and former railroad trestle as well as a series of dramatic ledges.

Hiram Falls, on the Saco River in Hiram, features a series of falls below the Central Maine Power Co. dam and power plant.

Holeb Falls, on the Moose River in Attean, includes two parallel falls and an eight-yard drop.

Howe Brook Falls, on Howe Brook (T5 R9 WELS), allows clear mountain water to cascade over pools, potholes, and chutes.

Houston Brook Falls, on Houston Brook in Pleasant Ridge, allows swimming below a series of falls.

Katahdin Stream Falls, on Katahdin Stream (T3 R10 WELS), includes four vertical drops in a mossy ravine.

Little Abol Falls, on Little Abol Stream in Mount Katahdin Township, is a scenic set of falls in the Baxter State Park area.

Little Allagash Falls, on Allagash Stream in Eagle Lake Township, can only be reached by boat, but includes a scenic four-yard drop.

Little Niagara Falls, on Nesowadnehunk Stream (T3 R10 WELS), is another pleasant four-yard cascade.

Little Wilson Falls, on Little Wilson Stream in Elliottsville Plantation, is one of the highest falls in Maine, with a thirteen-yard main drop.

Moxie Falls, on Moxie Stream in Moxie Gore, features a towering thirty-yard cascade.

Nesowadnehunk Falls, on the West Branch of the Penobscot River (T2 R10), allows superb views of Mount Katahdin.

Old Roll Dam, on the West Branch of the Penobscot River, is a nice two-yard drop over green slate.

Poplar Stream Falls, on Poplar Stream in Carrabassett Valley, includes two scenic falls and a swimming hole near one of the new Maine Huts & Trails backcountry lodges.

Redington Pond Falls, in Redington Township, includes a series of waterfalls that comprise a 107-yard total drop.

Rocky Brook Falls, on Rocky Brook (T15 R8 WELS), features two drops and the remains of Maine's log-driving days.

Rumford Falls, on the Androscoggin River in Rumford, features a fifty-nine-yard cascade over granite ledges.

Sawtelle Falls, on Sawtelle Brook (T6 R7 WELS), features a five-yard drop carved through a sandstone ledge.

Screw Auger Falls, on Gulf Hagas Stream in Bowdoin College Grant East, is known as Maine's Grand Canyon for its impressive series of drops in a narrow canyon.

Shin Falls, on Shin Brook (T6 R7 WELS), features three falls for a total drop of eighteen yards over red and green slate.

Slugundy Falls, on Long Pond Stream in Elliottsville, is situated in a scenic gorge near the Appalachian Trail.

Smalls Falls, on Sandy River in Township E, is a scenic spot at the junction of the Sandy River and Chandler Mill Stream.

Steep Falls, on the Saco River in Standish, features a two-yard drop near a former railroad bed and mill ruins.

Step Falls, on Wight Brook in Newry, is a safe bet if you're on a family trip, as it's not too difficult to reach. The view isn't shabby, either, with a total combined drop of forty-five yards over a series of channels and cascades.

Swift River Falls, on the Swift River in Roxbury, is a great choice if you prefer to pull over your car rather than pull on the hiking boots. The hydraulic granite sculpture and two drops don't hurt, either.

Tobey Falls, on Big Wilson Stream in Willimantic, includes three sets of falls and a plunge pool below the lower falls.

West Chairback Pond Falls, on West Chairback Pond Stream (T7 W9 NWP), is a scenic eighteen-yard drop near the Appalachian Trail.

White-Water Rafting

The center of the white-water rafting world in Maine is a tiny speck of a place called The Forks, at the confluence of the Dead and Kennebec rivers. More than a dozen rafting companies are headquartered here, in the heart of the North Woods, some forty-five miles north of Skowhegan on Route 201. (You'll also find outfitters in Bingham, Greenville, South China, Millinocket, and Fryeburg). Action on the Kennebec, Penobscot, and Dead rivers gets started as soon as the ice breaks up in April and continues right through October's spectacular foliage season. Some trips last for six hours; some for two or three days. Neophytes and families will probably want to choose one-day expeditions (priced between $50 and $129 per person). For names of additional rafting outfitters, contact local chambers of commerce.

Maine Whitewater, Inc., Bingham
Offering daily trips on the Kennebec, Dead, and Penobscot rivers. *800-345-6246. www.mainewhitewater.com*

Adventure Bound, Caratunk
Offering daily and multiple-day trips on the Kennebec River. *888-606-7238. www. adv-bound.com*

New England Outdoor Center, Caratunk and Millinocket
Offering single and multiple-day trips on the Kennebec, Dead, and Penobscot rivers. *800-634-7328. www.neoc.com*

Access to Adventure, Jackman
Offering trips from one day to one week on the Kennebec, Dead, and Penobscot rivers. *1800-864-2676. jackmanmaine.org/maine-rafting.php*

Windfall Outdoor Center, Jackman
Offering daily and multiple-day trips on the Kennebec and Dead rivers. *800-683-2009. www.windfallrafting.com*

Wilderness Expeditions, Inc., Rockwood
Offering daily and multiple-day trips on the Penobscot and Kennebec rivers. *800-825-9453. www.wildernessrafting.com*

Crab Apple Whitewater, Inc., The Forks
Offering single and multiple-day trips on the Kennebec and Dead rivers. *800-553-7238. www.crabappleinc.com*

Moxie Outdoor Adventures, The Forks
Offering single and multiple-day trips on the Kennebec, Dead, and Penobscot rivers. *800-866-6943. www.wild-rivers.com*

Northern Outdoors, The Forks
Offering single and multiple-day trips on the Kennebec, Dead, and Penobscot rivers. *800-765-7238. www.northernoutdoors.com*

Inn by the River's Outdoor Adventures, West Forks
Offering daily and two-day trips on the Kennebec River. *866-663-2181. www. innbytheriver.com*

North American Outdoor Adventure, West Forks
Offering daily and longer trips on the Kennebec and Dead rivers. *800-727-4379. www.americanwhitewater.com*

North Country Rivers, West Forks
Offering daily and multiple-day trips on the Penobscot, Kennebec, and Dead rivers. *800-348-8871. www.ncrivers.com*

Magic Falls Rafting Company, West Forks
Offering daily trips and multiple-day trips on the Kennebec and Dead rivers. *800-207-7238. www.magicfalls.com*

Professional River Runners of Maine, Inc., West Forks
Offering daily and multiple-day trips on the Kennebec, Dead, and Penobscot rivers. *800-325-3911. www.proriverrunners.com*

Three Rivers Whitewater, West Forks
Offering daylong and multiple-day trips on the Kennebec, Dead, and Penobscot rivers. *877-846-7238. www.threeriverswhitewater.com*

Paddling

Maine offers canoeists some of the best paddling in the East, and the Allagash and St. John rivers enjoy national reputations for their wildness and scenery. Of course, there are dozens more rivers to explore across the state, from raging rapids to placid flat water, running through extraordinarily beautiful terrain. The following is a sampling of some of the top trips possible, organized south to north, most of which are fairly easy. Several guidebooks are available to canoeing enthusiasts; among the best are the Appalachian Mountain Club's *River Guide: Maine* and DeLorme's *The Maine Atlas and Gazetteer*.

Saco River
Always popular, the lazy Saco River has become the beginner's Allagash. It's a great introduction to both paddling and canoe camping. Most people put in near Fryeburg and ride the gentle swells to Hiram, spending a night at one of a handful of public campsites on the sandy beaches along the way. The river winds through farm country and beneath western-mountain foothills, but it's also extremely popular (and

occasionally rowdy), so you might consider a trip during the week in high summer or sometime in the shoulder seasons. *www.mainelakeschamber.com*

Ossipee River
The Ossipee River provides the boundary between Oxford and York counties, and it also makes for a great little day trip by canoe. The put-in is in the village of Kezar Falls; from there the river flows almost directly east for eight miles to Cornish. The current is enough to tug you right along, and there are sections of easily navigable rapids. *www.oxfordhillsmaine.com*

Pemaquid River
One of the more pleasant places to dip a paddle in the midcoast is the Pemaquid River, a sleepy waterway that links saltwater Pemaquid Harbor with freshwater Boyd Pond. The surroundings change frequently, from quiet, woodsy stretches to wide-open marshes, and a wealth of wildlife can be seen — watch for turtles swimming below the surface of the clear water. There's good swimming all along the way, and canoe rentals are available at the put-in, which is just off Route 130, a few miles north of Pemaquid Point. *www.damariscottaregion.com*

Sheepscot River
Head Tide and Sheepscot are among Maine's prettiest villages, and the Sheepscot River is a big reason why. Salty and serene, it sways easily back and forth between the two through the bucolic town of Alna, and its banks are largely undeveloped. The paddling is simple enough for beginners, and there are easy places to put in — just south of Head Tide alongside Route 194 are grassy banks all but made for canoeists. *www.damariscottaregion.com*

East Machias River
The trip down the East Machias River can be as long or as short as you like. Multiple access points allow you to paddle for an afternoon or several days. There are a number of put-in points on the East Machias' headwaters, Pocomoonshine Lake, and the river flows through Crawford Lake, too, before it takes its own name and shape, so a lot of the going is on flat water. You can begin in the small Greater Calais town of Alexander and end in either Crawford or in an unpopulated township to the south. *www. machiaschamber.org*

Nezinscot River
You'd never know you were a short drive from one of Maine's biggest urban areas when you canoe the Nezinscot. A fairly quiet river, it parallels the Turner Road between Buckfield and Turner Center, not far from the city streets of Lewiston and Auburn, but the landscape is woodsy and pastoral. The going is straightforward on the twelve-mile route — any rapids you encounter are fairly simple. *www2. androscoggincounty.com/public/*

Moose River

For ambitious paddlers, the Moose River trip is a mini Allagash. But it's more convenient in that it uses interconnecting lakes and ponds to form a long multi-day loop, so there's no need for shuttles or multiple vehicles. It does require portages, though, some of which can be lengthy, and you should keep an eye to the wind, which can make crossing the big lakes hairy. The scenery is unparalleled, the camping remote, and often moose are your only companions. *www.kennebecvalley.org*

Nesowadnehunk Stream

Nesowadnehunk Stream runs along the western edge of Baxter State Park, offering canoeists extraordinary views of the famous park's legendary peaks. An expedition on it begins below a lake of the same name just outside the park's boundaries, and you then flow down to Baxter's Nesowadnehunk Field Campground. The trip is only five miles, but they are five very spectacular miles. *www.katahdinmaine.com*

Royal River

The Royal River is known to just about anyone who has ever driven Interstate 95. It's the small watercourse that goes under the road in Yarmouth. Go upstream and you'll find some paddling of the easy, meandering type. A fun six-mile run begins off Route 9 in North Yarmouth. *www.yarmouthmaine.org*

Androscoggin River

One of the state's most industrious waterways, the Androscoggin also provides the hydraulics for some great canoeing, especially the stretch from Bethel to Rumford. You can ride the river for some twenty miles on relatively placid water, through bold western mountain terrain, enjoying serene farm country. The put-in is off Route 2 in Bethel. *www.bethelmaine.com*

Aroostook River

Passable for more than a hundred miles, the Aroostook offers canoeists a look at a good chunk of the County. There are many good trips on the quiet, windy river, but one of the best is from tiny Ashland to Fort Fairfield, past Presque Isle and Caribou, a long and winding row. *www.fortcc.org*

Whale Watching

Bar Harbor Whale Watch, Bar Harbor

These fully narrated trips leave from 1 West Street at the town pier and tend to run about three and a half hours long. You may also be treated to the sight of dolphins, porpoises, and seals, as well, so don't forget the camera. Trips begin June 21 through August 20 at 1 P.M., August 21 through October 2 at 8:30 A.M. and 1 P.M., October 3 through late October at noon, and July 13 through August 21 at

4:30 P.M. $56 for adults, $28 for ages six to fourteen, $8 for kids five and under. *Call 207-288-2386 or visit www.barharborwhales.com for more information.*

Boothbay Whale Watch, Boothbay Harbor

Board the *Harbor Princess* on a leviathan quest, with trips narrated by a naturalist and an onboard galley serving hamburgers, hot dogs, and sandwiches. Trips are approximately three to four hours long, and if for some reason you don't sight any of the creatures, they'll issue you a standby pass (that doesn't expire) for another trip. Even if Moby Dick fails to show himself, you're sure to see seals, possibly a porpoise, and all types of flying creatures. There is one trip daily June 12 through July 2 at 11 A.M. and 12:30 on Sunday; from July 3 through September 5, trips are twice daily at 9:30 A.M. and 1:30 P.M., except on Sunday when there is only one trip at 12:30 P.M.; and from September 6 through October 10, there's one trip daily at 11 A.M. $38 for adults, $32 for eleven to sixteen, $25 for six to tens, and free for kids under five. *Call 207-633-3500 or 888-WHALEME for more information or visit www.whaleme.com*

Cap'n Fish's, Boothbay Harbor

Whales and other Maine marine wildlife abound beyond the rails of the *Pink Lady*, the *Pink Lady II*, or the *Island Lady*. Wildlife experts narrate the trips, which last between three and three-and-a-half hours. From July 3 to September 5 trips run twice daily Monday through Saturday at 9:30 A.M. and 1:30 P.M., and at 12:30 P.M. on Sunday. Starting September 6 until October 10, trips run daily at 11:30 A.M. except for Sundays, when they leave at 12:30 P.M. $38 for adults, $32 for children eleven to sixteen, $25 for children six to ten, and free for kids under five. Plus, there's a snack bar in case all that salt air makes you hungry. *Call 207-633-3244 or 800-636-3244 or visit www.mainewhales.com*

Eastport Windjammers, Eastport

The *Sylvina W. Beal*, a fifty-passenger windjammer out of Eastport, runs daily whale watching trips leaving at 1:30 P.M. and lasting until 4:30 P.M. Visit whale feeding grounds and admire the other creatures, such as porpoises, seals, and eagles, along the way. You may also catch a peek of the Old Sow, the largest whirlpool in the western hemisphere (don't worry, captains know to stay at a safe distance). $37 for adults, $20 for those twelve and under. *Call 207-853-2500 for more information or visit www.eastportwindjammers.com/beal.html*

Cape Arundel Cruises (Nautilus), Kennebunkport

One daily four-hour trip at 10 A.M. from Memorial Day through Columbus Day, plus a sunset whale watch in July and August. *Call 207-967-0707 or 877-933-0707.*

First Chance Whale Watch, Kennebunkport

Four to four and a half hour trips. From June 28 through September 12, daily departures are at 10 A.M. and noon on Sundays, and from September 13 through October 3, weekends only at 10 A.M. $48 for adults, $28 for children three to twelve, and $10 kids up to three. Call *207-967-5507 or 800-767-2628 or visit www.firstchancewhalewatch.com*

Seafari Charters, Kittery

Private charters aboard *Seafari* are available from April 1 until the end of November for up to twenty people for an hour of steaming time. The ride also includes an on-board mammal library and videotapes. $30 per person. Call *207-439-5068 or visit www.seafaricharters.com*

Atlantic Adventures, Portland

Whale watching, deep-sea fishing, and scenic cruises with lobstering. May 1 through October 15. Trips by reservation only. Call *207-838-9902 or visit www. atlanticadventures.biz*

Odyssey, Portland

This whale-watch cruise on Casco Bay leaves Long Wharf at 10 A.M. Cruises are June 10 through October 31, Monday, Tuesday, Thursday, and Friday at 10 A.M. The boat ride takes about six hours. Adults $47, children twelve and under $38, and infants two and under $9. Call *207-775-0727 or visit www.odysseywhalewatch.com*

Beaches

The Maine coast is famous for its pounding surf and jagged cliffs. But tucked along our shores are some fine, if sometimes tiny, stretches of sand where you can lay out a towel or wiggle your toes on a warm July afternoon. The following is a sampling of some of Maine's finest coastal beaches; more can be discovered in DeLorme's *Maine Atlas and Gazetteer* or by asking locals.

Crescent Beach, Kittery

Sandy swimming opportunity on a peninsula. *207-363-4422.*

Ogunquit Beach

White sand beach amid a booming resort community. One of the state's most scenic shores is this 3¹/₂-mile strip of sand famous for its swimming, its surfing, and its sandcastle-building. After sunbathing, take a walk on the nearby Marginal Way, Ogunquit's mile-long seaside trail (see page 48). *207-646-2939.*

Kennebunk Beach

Gently sloping sands in a sheltering cove, this beach is ideal for children. *207-967-0857.*

Mother's Beach, Kennebunk
This sheltered cove has gently sloping sands, lifeguards at the ready, and a nearby playground, all of which make the aptly named beach ideal for children. *207-967-0857.*

Ferry Beach, Saco
A favorite swimming spot with a park and picnic facilities. *207-282-4489.*

Old Orchard Beach
One of the busiest resort towns in Maine, it offers four miles of beachfront with a broad and gentle slope ideal for lounging and swimming. *207-934-5714.*

Crescent Beach, Cape Elizabeth
In addition to its gentle arc of sand this 243-acre state park, off Route 77, has a pleasant trail that loops through woods and fields. There are also picnicking facilities, a snack bar, and showers. *207-287-3821.*

Ferry Beach and Western Beach, Scarborough
Divided by a rocky point, these are sandy sister beaches, with a park and picnic facilities at Ferry Beach. *207-730-4000.*

Pine Point Beach, Scarborough
This beach starts at the narrow mouth of the Scarborough River, opposite Ferry Beach, and extends south to Old Orchard. Pine Point offers the added bonus of a boat landing. *207-730-4000.*

Scarborough Beach
This park near the end of Route 207, before you reach Prouts Neck, is popular with local families as well as younger Greater Portlanders who come for the surf and the sand. *207-883-2416.*

Higgins Beach, Scarborough
A sandy beach with fine swimming, albeit extremely limited parking. *207-730-4000.*

Popham Beach, Phippsburg
This beach sports a vast stretch of sand with tidal pools, dunes, and rocky outcroppings ideal for exploring. Surf-fishing for striped bass is a popular pastime here, and although the water can be on the chilly side, many enjoy a romp in these waves. *207-389-1335.*

Reid State Park, Georgetown
With plenty of beach between two rocky headlands, and broad views of islands and the open ocean, plus picnicking and camping facilities, this beach is one of the most frequented swimming areas along the midcoast. This 1.5-mile beach is broken into three distinct sections so you can take your pick. The water's nippy and the surf can

get rough, but fortunately for parents there's a warm-water lagoon for kids to safely splash around in. Another surfcasting hot spot at dawn and dusk. *207-371-2303.*

Lincolnville Beach
Always popular, this short stretch of sand lies in the very heart of midcoast Maine right on Route 1. *207-236-4404.*

Lamoine Beach
Part of Lamoine State Park, this pebble beach is a perennial favorite, with long views and plenty of room for exploration. *207-667-4778.*

Sand Beach, Mount Desert
Despite the chilly water temperatures, this small beach, tucked in between rocky outcroppings, is extremely popular on hot summer days. Trivia tidbit: Sand Beach was featured in the film version of *The Cider House Rules*. *207-288-3338.*

Roque Bluffs Beach
On the shores of Englishman Bay, this beach has facilities for both salt- and freshwater swimming. *207-255-3475.*

State Parks

State Parks To Walk

Vaughan Woods Memorial State Park is a 250-acre old-growth hemlock and pine forest with more than three miles of easy, inter-looping trails offering fine views of the Salmon Falls River and its cascades. The woods are home to bald eagles, turkey, and deer. *28 Oldfields Rd., South Berwick. 207-384-5160; 207-624-6080, off-season.*

Bradbury Mountain State Park, about fifteen miles north of Portland, is a great place to introduce children to hill hiking. At just 485 feet, Bradbury's bald summit offers youngsters a sense of accomplishment, thanks to the fine views of the surrounding countryside and Casco Bay. The hike is easily extended by following any one of a number of trails that meander through the park's eight hundred forested acres. *528 Hallowell Rd., (Rte. 9), Pownal. 207-688-4712.*

Little exertion is required to experience some of **Grafton Notch State Park**'s finest features, the deep gorges and cascades of Moose Cave, Mother Walker Falls, and Screw Auger Falls (how can you not check out places with such names?). The real hiking is up 4,170-foot Old Speck. The Old Speck Trail, which is part of the Appalachian Trail, is a strenuous eight miles, but you can break it up with an overnight stay at one of the campsites on Speck Pond, about a mile below the summit. *Rte. 26 between Upton and Newry. 207-624-6080.*

Camden Hills State Park is like Acadia National Park in miniature: thirty miles of trails, most of them steep enough to offer a respectable workout yet short enough to allow ample time for shopping and dining in Camden village that same afternoon. The views are stupendous, stretching from the village and its boat-filled harbor across island-dotted Penobscot Bay to the horizon (look for the trio of wind turbines spinning on North Haven thirteen miles out to sea). *Rte.1, Camden. 207-236-3109.*

Shackford Head State Park sits on an undeveloped headland that juts into Broad Cove, part of Cobscook Bay, famed for its extreme tides and wild coastline. A short, easy hiking trail passes through a pine and birch forest on its way to the promontory and views of Campobello Island, the summer retreat of President Franklin Delano Roosevelt. There are secluded beaches to discover and blueberries and blackberries to pick in the meadows. *Deep Cove Rd., Eastport. 207-941-4014.*

Holbrook Island Sanctuary is a prime birding destination in part because of its varied habitats — fir and hardwood forest, meadows, freshwater ponds, and saltwater marshes. Watch for land and shorebirds, as well as fox, otter, bobcat, and coyote, from three short hiking trails. Canoeists and kayakers paddle to the park's 115-acre island and to the reversing falls at nearby Goose Falls. *172 Indian Bar Rd., Brooksville. 207-326-4012.*

Quaggy Jo Mountain springs suddenly out of the potato fields of Presque Isle, and a hike to its 1,214-foot summit yields sweeping views. Sitting alongside Echo Lake, the mountain is the most prominent feature of Aroostook State Park, Maine's first state park and perhaps the one most actively engaged with its surrounding community, which enjoys it year-round. In winter, its four miles of trails are groomed for skiing. There is a swim area, boat launch, and campground. *87 State Park Rd., Presque Isle. 207-768-8341.*

State Parks to Splash

Waves are fun, but families with tots prefer placid water. These four family-friendly beaches offer smooth swimming and lifeguards, too.

1. **Range Ponds State Park Lower Range Pond**, one in a chain of three pretty, tree-lined ponds, boasts a long sandy beach. Amenities include bathhouses and picnic tables. *31 State Park Rd., Poland. 207-998-4104; 624-6080 off-season.*

2. **Peaks-Kenny State Park Ten-mile-long Sebec Lake**, the centerpiece of this heavily wooded 838-acre park, has a sandy beach on South Cove. Besides swimmers, Sebec draws canoeists and anglers. There is a small, wooded campground. *Rte. 153, Dover-Foxcroft. 207-564-2003; 207-941-4014 off-season.*

3. Damariscotta Lake State Park Just seventeen acres, Damariscotta Lake State Park has a fine sandy beach, a small playground, picnic tables, and grills. *Rte. 32, Jefferson. 207-549-7600; 207-941-4014 off-season.*

4. Mount Blue State Park When the kids tire of splashing in Webb Lake, you don't have to go far to find other activities to keep them busy: rent a kayak or paddleboat, hike Mount Blue, mountain bike or ride a horse in the Center Hill area, and attend ranger-led nature programs, all without leaving the park. *187 Web Beach Rd., Weld. 207-585-2347; 207-585-2261 off-season.*

Best Beach State Parks

Popham Beach State Park

Mercurial Popham looks different every year thanks to the ever-shifting Morse River. Always breathtaking, it has just about everything you could want in a beach: a three-mile stretch of fine white sand, warm tide pools deep enough for wading, boardwalks through dunes sprouting rugosa roses, and a small rocky island accessible at low tide. *Rte. 209, Phippsburg. 207-389-1335.*

Reid State Park

Reid State Park has two strands, distinctive for their coarse sand tinged red by grains of garnet and feldspar. Mile Beach and Half-Mile Beach are separated by a rocky headland offering sweeping views of islands, lighthouses, and fishing villages. There's a sheltered saltwater lagoon, too. *Rte. 127, Georgetown. 207-371-2303.*

Crescent Beach State Park

A favorite of Portland area residents, the fine white sand of Crescent Beach is a sweet, gently curving interlude in Maine's famously rugged coast. The waves are typically modest, which makes Crescent great for young children, but surfers like it when conditions are right. *Rte. 77, Cape Elizabeth. 207-799-5871.*

Ferry Beach State Park

Here's a beach where you can get out of the sun and stretch your legs and your mind on a ranger-led interpretive tour. About 1.5 miles of easy trails and boardwalks traverse this one hundred-acre park, whose signature feature is a stand of tupelo, or black gum trees, that are rare this far north. *95 Bayview Rd., Saco. 207-283-0067; 207-624-6080 off-season.*

Roque Bluffs State Park

Way Down East in the town of Roque Bluffs, this 274-acre park is remote, secluded, and utterly spectacular. A crescent-shaped pebble beach separates the ocean from a freshwater pond; swimmers enjoy dipping into both. The wildlife watching is great, and there are five walking trails of varying lengths. *145 Schoppee Point Rd., Roque Bluffs. 207-255-3475.*

Great State Parks for Boating

Motorboat. Sebago Lake State Park offers access to Maine's premier vacation lake, a power boater's paradise. Besides a boat launch, the park has a sandy beach, hiking trails, a picnic area, and a campground. *11 Park Access Rd., Casco. 207-693-6231.*

Daysailer. When the breeze is up, seven-mile long Rangeley Lake gives sailors a wave-skipping ride. Rangeley Lake State Park has a boat launch, grassy swim area, and hiking trails. *South Shore Dr., Rangeley. 207-864-3858; 207-624-6080 off-season.*

Paddleboat. Lake St. George is dotted with small beckoning islands, and Lake St. George State Park answers their calls by renting paddleboats, those festive — and a little bit silly — water bikes. There is a boat launch, swimming area, and campground (and canoe and kayak rentals, too). *278 Belfast Augusta Rd., Liberty. 207-589-4255.*

Kayak. Androscoggin Riverlands State Park, Maine's newest state park, offers paddling on a peaceful, island-dotted stretch of the Androscoggin. This unexpected 2,588-acre wilderness, where loons, ducks, and otter swim and moose graze in the shallows, is just a few miles north of Lewiston and Auburn. Still in development, Riverlands aims to offer a more rustic experience than most other state parks. *Center Bridge Rd., Turner. 207-624-6080.*

Canoe. Located in the heart of Maine's fabled North Woods, the Allagash Wilderness Waterway, a ninety-two-mile band of rivers, lakes, and streams, and the Penobscot River Corridor, with sixty-seven miles of river and seventy miles of lake frontage, are splendid destinations for canoe and camping trips. Escapes to these remote regions require careful planning. *For information, write to BPL at 106 Hogan Rd., Bangor, Maine 04401, or call 207-941-4014.*

Fun State Park Campsites

Every campground has a few tent sites that fill up almost as soon as the reservation office opens for the season. Here are popular picks at four parks beloved for camping. (BPL begins accepting reservations on February 1. Call 800-332-1501 or visit www.maine.gov/doc/parks/reservations.)

Campsite #101
Cobscook Bay State Park

You will haul your gear a couple of hundred feet to reach site 101, but the rewards are tranquility and views of Broad Cove. Also in high demand: sites 96, 124, and 125. If you can't snag them, don't despair. Cobscook, a staging ground for daytrips to Quoddy Head, Campobello Island, and other points in eastern Maine, has dozens of seaside spots. *40 South Edmunds Rd., Pembroke. 207-726-4412.*

Campsite #7
Warren Island State Park

If solitude is what you're seeking, it's hard to go wrong on seventy-acre Warren Island, accessible only by boat; site 7 just happens to be the most secluded of nine tent sites and two lean-tos. Be prepared to rough it: The park has no hot showers or flush toilets, and some days you won't even see a ranger, but the sunsets and bird watching are outstanding. *Off Lincolnville in Penobscot Bay. 207-941-4014.*

Campsite #62
Lamoine State Park

Site 62 edges out 56 through 61 because the camp road doesn't run between it and Frenchman's Bay. Otherwise, all seven of these relatively open plots are well sited, offering views of nearby Mount Desert Island. Lamoine is where Acadia National Park visitors who want a respite from the crowds bed down. *23 State Park Rd., Lamoine. 207-667-4778.*

Campsite #203
Lily Bay State Park

The truth is, all of this Moosehead Lake campground's thirty-five waterside sites are booked early for summer weekends. Number 203, along with 205, 208, 210, and 211, are preferred by folks who want easy access to their car. Number 41, alone on a peninsula at the end of a four hundred-foot path, is cherished by those with a different mindset. *13 Myrle's Way, Greenville. 207-695-2700.*

Perfect Park Picnic Spots

One of these beautiful settings plus delicious food cooked by someone else add up to a carefree picnic.

Two Lights State Park
66 Two Lights Rd., Cape Elizabeth. 207-799-5871
lobster rolls from the Lobster Shack (225 Two Lights Rd., Cape Elizabeth. 207-799-1677) raspberry shortbread squares from Scratch Bakery (416 Preble St.,

South Portland. 207-799-0668) = a simple meal in an exhilarating atmosphere: a windswept rocky headland pounded by surf.

Wolfe's Neck Woods State Park
426 Wolfe's Neck Rd., Freeport. 207-865-4465
Baby back ribs from Buck's Naked BBQ (568 U.S. Rte. 1, Freeport. 207-865-0600) cappuccino brownies from Simply Divine Brownies (7 Mill St., second floor, Freeport. 207-865-3961) = a hearty, finger-licking lunch that can be walked off on miles of wooded trails skirting Casco Bay and the Harraseeket River.

Birch Point State Park
Ballyhac Rd., Owl's Head. 207- 941-4014
burgers from the Owls Head General Store (2 South Shore Dr., Owl's Head. 207-596-6038) chocolate chip cookies from the Brown Bag (606 Main St., Rockland. 207-596-6372) = a juicy meal on a secluded, sandy beach, followed by some serious digestion time on sun-warmed granite slabs.

Moose Point State Park
310 West Main St. (Rte. 1),Searsport.
207-548-2882
spicy seafood noodles from Seng Thai Restaurant (160 Searsport Ave. (Rte. 1), Belfast. 207-338-0010) fudge from Perry's Nuthouse (45 Searsport Ave. (Rte. 1), Belfast. 207-338-1630) = an exotic repast in a shady fir grove, topped off with some tide-pooling on the shores of Penobscot Bay.

Swan Lake State Park
Rte. 141, Swanville.207-525-4404
Hawaiian sandwiches from Bell the Cat (Renys Plaza, 1 Belmont Ave., Belfast. 207-338-2084) fresh fruit from the Belfast Co-op (123 High St., Belfast. 207-338-2532) = a relaxing splash-and-eat day on a lake in the rolling hills north of Belfast.

State Park Lighthouses

Owls Head Lighthouse
Adjacent to Owls Head Light State Park, Owl's Head. *207-941-4014.*
Built: 1852
Height: 26 feet
Shape and color: cylindrical white brick tower with black lantern
Automated: 1989
Light sequence: fixed white
Range: 16 nautical miles
Fog horn signal: two blasts every twenty seconds

Worthy of note: recently restored, the lighthouse is Coast Guard property accessed through the state park and managed by the American Lighthouse Foundation

West Quoddy Head Light
Quoddy Head State Park, Lubec. *207-733-0911; 207-941-4014, off-season.*
Built: 1857
Height: 49 feet
Shape and color: cylindrical red and white striped brick tower
Automated: 1988
Light sequence: two seconds on, two seconds off, two seconds on, nine seconds off
Range: 8 nautical miles
Fog horn signal: two blasts every thirty seconds
Worthy of note: West Quoddy Head Light is the only candy-striped lighthouse in the country

Fort Point Lighthouse
Fort Point State Park, Route 1, Stockton Springs. *207- 567-3356.*
Built: 1857
Height: 31 feet
Shape and color: white square brick tower
Automated: 1988
Light sequence: fixed white
Range: 15 nautical miles
Fog horn signal: one blast every 10 seconds
Worthy of note: Fort Point Light is the only lighthouse in Maine that has a round brick lining and circular stairway within a square exterior

45 Adventures in Maine

1 Make Way for Moose
Designated both a state scenic highway and a national scenic byway, Route 201 from Skowhegan to Jackman — a.k.a. Moose Alley— is spectacular in autumn, with stunning ridge-top views and leisurely curves through river valleys. Create a 5.5-hour loop with Routes 6 and 150, which will sweep you along Moose River and the west shore of Moosehead Lake. Don't be so captivated by the views that you fail to keep an eye out for the North Wood denizens who give this route its nickname.

2 Step Back in Time
Maine has plenty to offer history buffs — our maritime museums alone are enough for a full vacation — but the Museums of Old York offer perhaps the highest concentration of historic exhibits in the state. From the Old Gaol, with its photo-

inducing pillory out front, to Jefferds' Tavern and John Hancock Warehouse, you'll think you've stepped right off the Turnpike and into the seventeenth century. *207-363-4974, www.oldyork.org*

3 Play Bridge Tender

If there are any youngsters around, you probably ought to let them press the button to raise the bridge in Perkins Cove. But if you happen to be all alone and a yacht needs to pass under this Ogunquit landmark, the crew will need you to work the bridge controls for them. And can you think of a more beautiful place by the sea to sit and wait for one to come along?

4 Set sail

July days are lovely when you're the captain of your own ship, but Maine sailors know that the freshest breezes arrive in September and October. In Penobscot Bay, fall usually finds the northwesterlies sweeping off the auburn-colored Camden Hills, making for great sailing and calm seas. Camden has the highest concentration of day-sailing schooners in the state, with ships and crews that will satisfy the needs of every traveler, whether you're looking for a way to take Fido sailing, listen to some sea stories, or just kick back and enjoy the wind on your face. *207-236-4404, www. camdenme.org*

5 Eat Indian Pudding

Indian pudding is not the most appetizing-looking dessert — it's mush, frankly — but its warm, molasses-y goodness, combined with a scoop of vanilla ice cream, quickly wins over anyone fond of old-fashioned sweets like grapenut pudding and gingerbread cake. Made with cornmeal, molasses, milk, ginger, and other spices, this nineteenth-century staple is not easy to find on today's menus. Look for it in restaurants specializing in classic Maine food, like the Maine Diner in Wells, Cole Farms in Gray, Le Garage in Wiscasset, and Moody's Diner in Waldoboro.

6 Scramble up Tumbledown

With its fine vistas, three peaks, big cliffs, and alpine pond, 3,068-foot Tumbledown Mountain easily ranks high on any Maine hiker's bucket list. Those features, along with Fat Man's Misery — a narrow, vertical conduit through some boulders — make this Weld-area massif an especially fun hike. To experience Fat Man's Misery, take the challenging Loop Trail. If you want less of a workout, follow the Brook Trail, an old logging road with a short, steep finish. We prefer to make a loop out of the two.

7 Fish On!

Overfishing has pretty much decimated groundfish stocks (as well as fishing fleets) in Maine, but recently reports have started trickling in about a gradual recovery happening in the Gulf of Maine. Captain James Harkins, who runs deep-sea fishing and whale-watching excursions from Portland aboard his Atlantic Adventurer, says his guests are hauling in larger fish than they have in decades. "Four or five years ago, we were lucky to see seven- or eight-pound fish," Harkins says. "Last week we pulled in a fifty-two-pound cod. We're seeing huge fish again." Set up your own fish tale. *207-838-9902, www.atlanticadventures.biz*

8 Run, Walk, or Relay
The largest long-distance running race in the state is the Maine Marathon, Relay, and Half-Marathon, planned in Portland. Better still, the event has raised $2.5 million in donations that benefit Maine charities and cancer research. Whether you can only do a couple of miles or else decide to tackle 13.1 or even the full marathon, you'll feel good after this event in so many ways. It's even fun to just be a spectator! *207-749-9160, www.mainemarathon.com*

9 Raise a Glass
The Maine coastline and countryside is becoming a perfect pairing for tasty and sophisticated wine. Some of the latest arrivals include Oyster River Wine Growers (*www.oysterriverwinegrowers.com*) in Warren, Breakwater Vineyards (*www.breakwatervineyards.com*) in Owl's Head, and Maine Mead Works (*mainemeadworks.com*) in Portland (not technically a winery, but its delicious honey mead is close enough in our book). Vineyard-hop on your own or check out the official Maine Wine Trail (*www.mainewinetrail.com*) and explore the different regions of Maine while sampling some amazing libations along the way.

10 Amble Down East
Located in the Donnell Pond Unit, a 14,162-acre wilderness managed by the Bureau of Parks and Lands, Schoodic Mountain is the highest in a cluster of mountains east of Ellsworth, and its bare, rocky summit yields views of sparkling ponds and the ocean. From the Donnell Pond Unit parking lot, take the trail that heads west to the summit. Add variety to your descent by taking the beach trail about 0.4 miles below the summit. You'll end up at Donnell Pond, where you can swim before returning to your car a half-mile down the trail. This moderate round-trip hike is 2.3 miles.

11 Add a Notch on Your Belt
The foliage can't get more dazzling than it does on Route 113, which runs from Fryeburg and Gilead through the White Mountain National Forest (you'll actually be in New Hampshire for a few miles). The narrow section that climbs through Evans Notch, a true mountain road that is closed in winter, is especially beautiful. There are a few pullouts where you can stop and soak it all in. Make a day of it by hiking Caribou, Speckled, or East and West Royce mountains. Or take a quick half-mile jaunt up the Roost and bask in the views of the Wild River Valley.

12 Run for the Border

More than two thirds of Maine shares a border with Canada, and yet few people get to experience what it's like to clear customs on almost a daily basis and have English as a second language. Lubec offers the opportunity to sleep in the U.S., visit an international park (Campobello), and have a meal in New Brunswick, all in a single day. You'll be counting your loonies before you know it! *207-733-2201, cobscookbay.com*

13 Get Campy

If you're not into the on-the-dirt type of North Woods camping, the rustic cabins at the Birches Resort in Rockwood offer a great way to get close to Mother Nature — without getting too close. The resort offers top-notch cuisine in its dining hall, and if you want to sample the latest in woods accommodations, there are even yurts available. *800-825-9453, www.birches.com*

14 Take in the View

The hoopla associated with the opening of the Penobscot Narrows Observatory in 2007 has died down, but the view from the bridge (one pylon contains the only one of these observatories in the United States) remains as breath-taking as ever. That's especially true on a clear autumn afternoon, when you can see from Katahdin to Deer Isle. *www.penobscotnarrowsbridge.com*

15 See the Light

Maine is for lovers — lighthouse lovers, that is. And one of the most unique lighthouse tours offered in the state is the three-hour excursion offered to Burnt Island Light, just off Boothbay Harbor. Interpreters dressed in period clothing explain the history of the light and the many keepers' families who have lived there, and naturalists lead walks around the five-acre island explaining the flora and fauna that survive so far out to sea. Tours are scheduled into early September. *207-633-2284, balmydayscruises.com/lighthouse*

16 Blast Away

As long as you've got the shoulder for it, there's something deeply satisfying about blasting away at a few dozen clay pigeons. The guides at L.L. Bean's Walk-On Adventures are masters at making sure the pigeons fly straight, the twelve gauge is always pointed in the right direction, and a smile is always on your face (oh, and the earplugs are always in, too!). At just twenty bucks for a ninety-minute session, this is one of the cheapest blasts in Maine. *800-441-5713, www.llbean.com*

17 Climb a Rock

You don't need to be Sir Edmund Hillary to scale a cliff, and the guides at the Atlantic Climbing School will tailor a daytrip in Camden to your physical ability and particular need for an adrenaline rush. With routes ranging from fifty feet to a couple of hundred, the cliffs at Barrett's Cove will give you a taste of life on the edge. And when you're done, a refreshing dip in Megunticook Lake is literally just a few steps away. *207-288-2521, www.climbacadia.com/camden*

18 Test the Tide

The coming and going of the tide is mesmerizing practically anywhere on the Maine coast, but without doubt one of the coolest places to experience it is at Bar Island in Frenchman's Bay. At low tide a sandbar reveals itself between downtown Bar Harbor and this tiny island, technically part of Acadia National Park, and you can actually drive a car out to the island (although we've watched brand-new pickups swamped and ruined forever by seawater). But the intertidal zone is really best experienced on foot, so check your tide charts and plan on spending a couple of hours on the island. Just don't get stuck — the tide comes in surprisingly quickly, and low tide won't return again for another twelve hours!

19 Put in a Paddle

Kayaks were made for Maine. With its rocky coastline and thousands of islands, bays, and rivers, the Pine Tree State is a paddling paradise. One of the best short excursions is the Pemaquid River near Damariscotta. In just the 2.5-mile stretch from the boat launch in Bristol Mills to Biscay Pond you're likely to see great blue herons, turtles, and dragonflies galore. If you don't have your own boat, Maine Kayak in New Harbor can rent you a kayak for a half-day or more. *866-624-6352.*

20 Settle an Argument

What makes the best preparation for fried clams? Should they be rolled in egg and breadcrumbs? Or dipped in light batter? The debate rages on. Weigh in at Harraseeket Lunch, a classic lobster shack on South Freeport Harbor that serves both varieties of the crunchy golden mollusks — whole belly, of course. Be sure to save room for the coconut cream pie. *207-865-4888. www.harraseeketlunchandlobster.com*

21 Discover the Back Roads

Most visitors to Maine's midcoast never stray from the shore, which is too bad because the rolling, pond-dotted countryside of Union, Hope, and Lincolnville is gorgeous. For a fine introduction to this bucolic area, follow Route 235 from Waldoboro to Lincolnville, then pick up Route 173 to Lincolnville Beach. Take Route 1 back to Waldoboro, and be sure to allow time for a drive up Mount Battie in Camden Hills State Park. The views of Penobscot Bay are jaw-dropping.

22 Scale a Baby White

Besides the masses of blueberries for which it is named, Blueberry Mountain, off Route 113 near the tiny town of Stow in western Maine, offers other pleasures. At 1,781 feet, Blueberry is modest by White Mountain standards, but its open ridges afford big views. Climb via the White Cairn Trail and descend on the Stone Ridge Trail so you can end your 4.5-mile journey by dipping your hot, weary feet in icy Rattlesnake Pool.

23 Hit the Slopes (Sans Snow)

The activities at Maine's tallest ski mountain are great year round. A fall weekend getaway to Sugarloaf can entail many adventures, not to mention gorgeous foliage vistas. Hop on the dozens of miles of mountain biking and hiking trails for free. Take a moose cruise to spot Maine's giant creatures in the surrounding forests. Or sign up for a Weekend Golf Tune Up and get two hours of individual instruction, a round of golf, accommodations, and lunch. Feeling jumpy? Whatever you do, don't miss the Antigravity Complex, a pepped-up gym with skateboarding venues. Nine dollars will get you an hour group lesson on the public trampoline! *207-237-2000, www. sugarloaf.com*

24 Meet The Greatest Mountain

The air is clear, the temperatures are moderate, and the foliage is outstanding: Now is the best time to scale Katahdin, which means "Greatest Mountain" in the Penobscot Indian language. At 5,267 feet, Maine's highest peak is not an easy climb. Plan on eight to ten hours and nearly 3,000 feet of near-vertical climbing. If you're not fit enough for The Greatest, you can get a taste for it on some of the shorter hikes in Baxter State Park or simply appreciate its imposing presence from a canoe on Daicey Pond. *207-723-5140, www.baxterstateparkauthority.com*

25 Take in a Waterfall

At eighty-nine feet, Moxie Falls has been rated the highest waterfall in New England. Located in Moxie Gore near The Forks (where the Kennebec and the Dead rivers join), it is a place of astounding beauty that requires little effort of the hiker. From the parking area on Moxie Lake Road, a short, wide path leads to a boardwalk at the top of the waterfall. Follow the boardwalk along the wooded gorge to a viewing platform overlooking the lower falls downstream. Numerous pools below the cascades make for great swimming.

26 Range Around Rangeley

Routes 4 and 17, which wrap like a loose scarf around Rangeley Lake, are designated a scenic byway by both the Maine Department of Transportation and the United States Federal Highway Administration. The route ascends the Appalachian Mountain ridgeline before dropping into a series of rolling valleys and hills. The Height of Land on Route 17, with its stunning views of Mooselookmeguntic Lake, is the road's showstopper.

27 Eat Lobster

Any time is a great time to hit up some of Maine's most popular lobster shacks. And there is no more beautiful a spot than the Lobster Shack, which is open until through October. The restaurant is adjacent to Two Lights State Park in Cape Elizabeth, offering one of the best accessible rocky coastlines in the state. Dining on a steaming Maine lobster at a picnic table on the rocks with crashing surf just a few feet away is a quintessential Maine activity. *207-799-1677, www.lobstershacktwolights.com*

28 Get Wild in Portland

Escape the noise and bustle of Maine's largest city without ever leaving its borders by venturing into the Fore River Sanctuary, an eighty-five-acre preserve of salt and freshwater marsh and red oak and pine forest. Managed by Portland Trails, the sanctuary is home to Portland's only natural waterfront, as well as the site of the former Cumberland and Oxford Canal. *207-775-2411, www.trails.org*

29 Take a Drive Back in Time

Beginning in the bayside city of Belfast — home to a lovely arts and restaurant scene — Route 7 eventually winds its way to the central Maine town of Newport on the shores of Sebasticook Lake and beyond to its ultimate destination of Dover-Foxcroft. Along the way the small, old-fashioned towns of Brooks and Dixmont give this drive an authentic country vibe. But the most distinguishing trait of the twenty-eight-mile stretch between Belfast and Plymouth is the rolling hills, which offer stunning views of the surrounding landscape. Also known as the Moosehead Trail, Route 7 possesses one of the coolest causeways in the state: Stop in at the roadside strip of sand at Plymouth Pond to put in a canoe or kayak or just to soak up some rays of sun.

30 Islander for a Day

There is an undeniable fascination with islands and the people who live on them, and Maine is fortunate enough to have more than a dozen islands that support year-round populations. One of the easiest and most pleasant islands where you can get a taste of life offshore while still retreating back to your bed on the mainland is Vinalhaven, at the mouth of Penobscot Bay. The first ferry from Rockland leaves at 7 A.M.; plan to be there with your bicycle. You'll be in Carvers Harbor in an hour and a quarter, leaving plenty of time for a ride around the island, a bag lunch on Lane's Island, and maybe even a dip in one of the abandoned quarries. Just make sure you don't get so relaxed that you miss the last boat home at 4:30 P.M.!

31 Visit the Pine Barrens in Autumn

Given its scruffy, coniferous name, colorful foliage is about the last thing you'd expect to find at the Waterboro Pine Barrens, a preserve managed by the Nature Conservancy. But interspersed with the green needles of the peculiar pitch pines are the glowing yellow-orange leaves of scrub oaks. Spread across several acres are wild blueberry bushes, which turn crimson in fall. The serene preserve, one of the largest such pine barrens in the world, boasts nearly fifteen miles of walking trails. *www.nature.org*

32 Make Cider

Fall is a great time to head out Route 26 in New Gloucester to the Shaker Village at Sabbathday Lake. Throughout the fall, this religious community twenty-five miles outside of Portland hosts several Apple Saturdays (call to check for dates) where you can bring your own apples or purchase Shaker apples from the orchard across the road. The folks there will press the apples for free to create your very own batch of cider. Plus there will be plenty of apple pie, candied apples, and cider doughnuts on hand depending on the date. *207-926-4597, www.maineshakers.com*

33 Drink Moxie

Created by a Maine man in the late nineteenth century, Moxie was first marketed as a "nerve food" effective in the treatment of insomnia and nervousness. The soft drink ultimately proved so popular that its name became associated with verve and derring-do. Now it's hard to find the soda outside New England. Some people love it; others hate it. How about you? Many Maine groceries carry it, but we'd be remiss if we didn't mention the Kennebec Fruit Company, 2 Main Street, Lisbon Falls, which has a small museum dedicated to the bitter stuff. *207-353-8173.*

34 Walk the Bog

The Bog Walk in Orono provides a great venue for taking contemplative strolls. Take a scheduled, guided nature tour or meander through the 616-acre wetland yourself via the wooden boardwalk, which is handicapped accessible. More than one hundred species of birds have been spotted in the bog, so be sure to bring your binoculars. *www.oronobogwalk.org*

35 Peruse Poland Spring

Poland Spring is known for its crystalline water, but we wouldn't recommend driving through without stopping for a burger and sweet potato fries at Cyndi's Dockside Restaurant & Boathouse, open year-round. Part of the Poland Spring Resort, this small lakeside joint located at Middle Range Causeway has all kinds of tasty seafood and snack options. But the burger reigns supreme — local meat from nearby Harvest Hill Farm is packed into a thin but satisfying patty grilled to perfection. And the sweet potato fries are addictive. Just make sure to rent one of the boats (preferably a person-powered one) afterwards to work it off! *207-998-5008, www.dockside.me*

36 Bowl Some Strings

Bowling has finally returned to Portland's peninsula. Former state representative Charlie Mitchell and State Senator Justin Alfond are behind Bayside Bowl on Alder street. The alley boasts twelve lanes of ten-pin bowling and a restaurant-bar that serves lunch, dinner, and weekend brunch, and often features live music events or a DJ. *207-761-2695, www.baysidebowl.com*

37 Boldly Go to Cutler

The Cutler Coast Public Reserved Land is an amazing stretch of Bold Coast, close to five miles of shoreline in Cutler. The cliffs plunge one hundred feet to an angry sea, the woods are quiet and serene, there are several hidden coves and pebble beaches, and the views out to Grand Manan and the village of Cutler are to die for. Better still, much of the time you can have it all to yourself. Take the Coastal Trail along the cliffs and loop through meadows and scruffy heath. There is nothing else in Maine quite like it. *www.maine.gov/doc/parks/programs/prl.html*

38 Roam Around the County

Settled by French-Acadians in the nineteenth-century, the St. John Valley is traversed by Route 11, a designated state scenic byway. From Portage to Fort Kent, the landscape provides travelers with unparalleled views of grasslands, wildflower meadows, the Fish River, Eagle Lake, and Maine's highest peak, Katahdin.

39 Pick Your Own Apples

Come autumn, the supermarket is no match for Maine's orchards, where the apples couldn't be crisper if you picked them yourself — and you can do just that because pick-your-own orchards abound. Some of our favorites include Apple Farm in Fairfield, which specializes in antique varieties like Grey Pearmain, and Thompson's Orchards in New Gloucester, beloved for its warm apple dumplings and doughnuts. For a list of orchards around the state, visit the Maine Pomological Society's Web site, *www.Maineapples.org*

40 Take a Foodie Tour

Comedian Randy Judkins, founder of the Maine Hysterical Society, is one of several excellent tour leaders offering a highly entertaining guided visit to some of Portland's most delicious food spots via Maine Foodie Tours. On the itinerary: beer, blueberries, crabmeat, and other Maine staples. Opt for a walking tour or hop on the trolley — either way you'll get a glimpse of Maine's largest city while dining on state delicacies. *207-233-7485, www.mainefoodietours.com*

41 Shop for Antiques

Nearly thirty antiques shops do business in the one-half square mile that comprises Wiscasset's beautiful riverfront village, an antique in its own right. You'll find all the vintage china, furniture, and assorted decorative objects that you'd expect from an antiques destination, along with a wide array of unusual items, like French peasant smocks and music boxes. There are four history museums in town, too. *www. shopwiscassetantiques.com*

42 Wander about an Island

Great Wass Island is a Nature Conservancy preserve consisting of 1,540 acres of boreal forest and rocky coast off Jonesport. Bird watchers come here to spot species like boreal chickadees and spruce grouse at the southern limit of their ranges. By piecing together the Little Cape Point Trail and the Mud Hole Trail, you can create a challenging and amazingly varied hike that skirts forest, bog, and shore. The parking area is Duck Cove on the island. *www.nature.org*

43 Say Moo!

Fall isn't complete without a visit to an old-fashioned agricultural fair, a celebration of the bountiful harvest and Maine's farming heritage. Windsor and Blue Hill kick the season off with festivals in late August and early September, followed by fairs in Oxford, Farmington, and Cumberland. The best known are the Fryeburg Fair, a traditional celebration with harness races, ox pulls, a midway, and loads of fried dough, and the Common Ground Fair, whose emphasis on organic farming, wholesome foods, and sustainable living sets it apart.

44 Go Back in Time

Two hundred years ago, Lemuel Moody scanned Casco Bay for vessels from atop the eighty-six-foot Portland Observatory and flew their colors to alert ship owners and merchants on the wharves below of their pending arrival. The only such maritime signal tower still standing in the United States, the observatory is now a museum with spectacular views. Take a tour, then head down Munjoy Hill to Portland's Eastern Cemetery to see the side-by-side tombs of two young sea captains, one American and one British, who perished in a battle near Monhegan Island and were buried in a joint funeral during the War of 1812. *207-774-5561, www.portlandlandmarks.org*

45 Explore the Two Acadias

Acadia National Park is stunning any time of year. Make a day of it with a driving tour that combines Acadia's two homes, Mount Desert Island and the Schoodic peninsula. Skim MDI's shoreline on Routes 3 and 102, branching off for a swing around the park Loop Road, one of the finest foliage drives in the nation. Follow Route 3 off the island and head east on Route 1 to Gouldsboro. Whether you choose Pond Road or Route 186, you'll be treated to views of coves, ponds, blueberry barrens, and mossy heaths on your way to your smashing finale — Acadia's quiet Schoodic District.